T0372269

STYLE STUDY

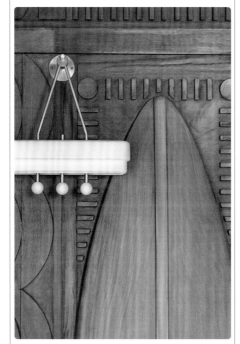

THIS BOOK BELONGS TO

....

THIS BOOK IS DEDICATED TO MY HUSBAND PHIL. ALWAYS.

LAUREN LI

BEACHSIDE MODERN

BEACHSIDE MODERN IS ...

SUMMERY

BRIGHT

FRESH

NOSTALGIC

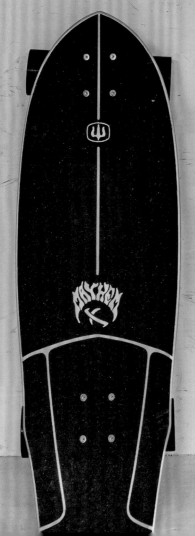

SERENE

Photographer COURTESY OF FERM LIVING

WELCOME

Our homes are an expression of who we are and how we live. They reflect our creativity, our quirks and interests, our style. I'm always intrigued by the stories that these spaces tell.

As a designer, I admire many interior styles but, as important as the *look* of a space is, often it's the *feel* of a space that draws me. The way design elements – the architecture, the furnishings, artworks and decor objects, and the surrounding environment – combine to create spaces with a feel-good factor.

In the Style Study series, I examine design across styles, genres and geographies, seeking out eye-catching homes from around the world and sharing the key elements of interior design, so you can bring your own style to life.

Beachside Modern explores coastal interior design across geographic regions to reveal five diverse beach looks – Nautical, Natural, Winter, Elevated and Beachcomber – and how to achieve that beach feel in our own homes. We take a deep dive into some of the best beach houses in the world, from the effortless Californian aesthetic of Commune Design and the soft minimalism of Danish designers Norm Architects to the understated grandeur of Athena Calderone's Amagansett home and the curated ramshackle of Sarah Andrews's evocative Tasmanian shack. With its focus on the core elements of coastal design, this book can guide you to capture those beach vibes for your home.

Part I, Coastal Vibes, uncovers the essence of beach style and the design features that underpin each look: from the impact of indoor/outdoor living to the use of colour and the selection of furnishings in creating a relaxed space. In Part II, Defining Your Beach Style, you'll start to identify your ideal coastal style and the look that works best for you. There are tips and tools to build a design plan so you can confidently shape your own beach-inspired interiors.

I'd love to think these stylish spaces will encourage you to create your own seaside haven, whether there's a beach on your doorstep or just in your dreams.

Founding Director, Sisällä Studio, Melbourne
LAUREN LI

I.

Photographer CRICKET SALEH

Interior Designer
GEORGINA JEFFRIES

This array of beachy items near the front door looks homely and welcoming. It's obvious that cool beach-lovers live here.

TIP   This arrangement works because the materials are united. Stash the fluoro goggles in the drawer.

COASTAL VIBES

The beach is a part of everyday living or holiday dreaming in countries around the world. Lazy days spent reading books on the sand under the shade of a colourful sun umbrella. Dipping in and out of the sea when the sun gets too hot. Losing all track of time until the sun slips below the horizon. Simply being near the water – or better still, in it – makes us feel beautifully free and relaxed.

No wonder so many of us want to bring the holiday feeling home from the beach and enjoy it every day. Wouldn't it be great if we could create that tranquil vibe in our own homes? I think we can. Just as the beach can cleanse and heal us, our homes can do this for us too.

Growing up in Mount Eliza, a quiet coastal village on Victoria's Mornington Peninsula, I took the beach for granted; it was just always there. Often, I'd walk the sandy trails barely noticing the view. I was looking at the houses instead – and glimpsing the interiors through large picture windows.

The Mornington Peninsula holds an array of coastal architecture ranging from modest beach cottages and charming mid-century homes to chunky split-level 1980s brick houses and, more recently, cutting-edge big box residences. It's also home to some design classics, like the 'Round House' by renowned architect Roy Grounds – an exercise in pure geometry.

The Peninsula is where my passion for design really began. Working there as an interior designer, I encountered small beach houses nestled into the tea trees at St Andrews Beach, sprawling Hamptons-style homes on clifftop estates and everything in between. I realised that my favourite beach homes are characteristically unpretentious and laid-back, they say something about the people who live there, and they're connected to the surrounding environment.

Beachside Modern analyses interior design across five distinct coastal styles, each with a relaxed, casual ambience and its own beachside flavour. Nautical uses fresh, clean colour; Natural embraces a relaxed, organic beach feel; Winter is inspired by the seasonal beauty of a chilly beach; Elevated creates a refined, aspirational look; and Beachcomber takes a rustic, eclectic approach to beachside living.

Across these beach house styles we'll unpack the materials used, complementary furnishings and decor, the layout, and how interior spaces connect to the outside – an essential component in creating a relaxed lifestyle. Whether you are building your beach house from the ground-up, renovating your home or decorating your rental apartment, the coming chapters present ideas and visions to help you create a beach style that is truly yours.

And if you don't live close to a beach at all? Don't worry, I believe that you can capture the spirit of the beach absolutely anywhere!

Interior Designer
DOROTHÉE DELAYE
STUDIO

This outdoor dining space at Hossegor on the west coast of France feels private and protected, yet allows views of the water to be enjoyed.

WHAT MAKES A GREAT BEACH HOUSE?

There is something captivating about a beach house, no matter where in the world you live. What is it about beachside living that makes us feel so relaxed and restored? I think the answer lies in the beach itself. Just as the beach leaves us with a physical imprint – salt-sprayed hair and sun-kissed skin – the beach house leaves an emotional imprint on our hearts and minds. It represents a break from the everyday grind, the rush of daily obligations, meetings and traffic jams. It gives us permission to breathe out and switch off.

For me, the best beach houses take inspiration from nature and capture the essence of how it *feels* to be at the beach. And while many houses reference the colours and textures of the beach, the truly great ones distil the raw natural beauty of the beach. They reflect the open spaces that remind us of crisp, clean air, the way that light falls, the water glistening. They observe the tidal shorelines that reveal earthy prehistoric rock formations hiding beneath pristine sands.

This relationship with nature has informed my approach to selecting the coastal residences profiled in this book, whether a quiet luxurious room that evokes the feeling of calm waters or a cold-climate seaside home that radiates warmth and protects against the elements. They are homes that seek a balance with their environment, connect indoor and outdoor spaces, and create a relaxed ambience for their occupants.

BALANCE IN NATURE

Beach houses with true impact, with restorative powers of calm and tranquility, connect with their surrounding environment. Especially those built specifically to respond to their location. There is rich variety in coastal architecture and interior styles around the world, typically reflected in the local vernacular, which is based on regional features, climate and customs. And there are inspiring houses in coastal locations across the globe.

Scandinavian countries have a long tradition of the summer house. They are revered places, often set in secluded locations that are immersed in nature. These sought-after rustic getaways (half the population has one and the other half wants one!) eschew new gadgets and multiple rooms for a simple, homely aesthetic that evokes a sense of childhood nostalgia.[1]

In New Zealand, the 'bach' – short for bachelor pad – has a special place in the hearts of many Kiwis. Originating in the early 1900s as simple fishing shacks in remote areas, they were built by fishermen and constructed from locally sourced materials.[2] Today, modest baches still offer back-to-basics holidays and are treasured for their authenticity, humble amenities and closeness to nature.

The way it responds to its location, and evokes the feeling of the beach in the house, can lift the experience of living in such a home, no matter if it's a modest seaside cottage or a mansion in an upscale beachside region.

In showcasing beach house interiors around the world, I want to share the diversity of these homes so you can find a style that speaks to you. It might be a rustic weatherboard cottage perched on the edge of the sea in Tasmania that draws you in; or a cool, laid-back Californian family home filled with arts and books.

Perhaps the allure of a luxe waterside home, its interior fitted with glamorous furniture, overlooking the sparkling Sydney Harbour will appeal; or a minimal Danish beach house where Japanese Zen meets Scandinavian charm.

When planning your beach look, consider the prevailing climate and the natural features of your locale. How can these be incorporated into your design for maximum benefit and impact?

BRINGING THE OUTDOORS IN

Beaches vary wildly in their locations and geography, from far-flung tropical paradise to urban coast, and rocky adventure playgrounds to flat white expanses. They host myriad forms of life – shells, seaweed, coral, fish and other sea life. They contain caves, pools and sand dunes, and every morning fresh treasures are strewn on the shore.

The beach is a source of infinite inspiration for design concepts that we can translate into our homes. In a beach-inspired house we want to evoke the spirit of the ocean, even if there isn't a drop of water in sight, and create a coastal atmosphere in the space.

This may be achieved through using local materials, such as quarried stone underfoot, or features like large open doors that lead to a patio dotted with sun loungers. It could be in found objects displayed on a shelf, such as driftwood and shells; in references to sand, water or rocks; or intangible elements like expansiveness, freshness and a salty air breeze.

LAID-BACK VIBES

Beach house style is about bringing a laid-back ethos to the way we live; it's comfortable, easy and unpretentious. Although the look is uncomplicated, it takes effort, consideration and time to achieve the loose kind of luxury that a beach house embodies.

While beach styles differ from place to place, there are consistent elements that help create a coastal vibe and the feeling of sun-bleached freedom that lovers of the beach house style desire.

Photographer ANSON SMART

Architect
TOBIAS PARTNERS

A series of oversized glass sliding doors means that indoors can truly merge with outdoors. On the upper level a freestanding bath can be seen behind a simple steel balustrade.

TIP   For maximum openness, use the largest sliding doors you can. Not only are they more seamless than bi-fold doors, they 'disappear' when they slide over each other.

BEACHSIDE MODERN ESSENTIALS

RAWNESS

Tones and grains of wood that reflect the colour of nature.

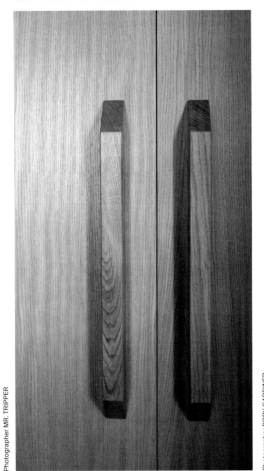

Photographer MR. TRIPPER

Interior Designer
DOROTHÉE DELAYE STUDIO

LIGHT

Large open windows to create a fresh, expansive feel.

Photographer RORY GARDINER

Interior Designer
PANDOLFINI ARCHITECTS

COLOUR

Monochromatic or tonal
colour palettes.

Photographer ANSON SMART

Interior Designer
ALEXANDER & CO

Stylist
CLAIRE DELMAR

TEXTURE

Natural materials like rattan, wool,
linen and stone.

Photographer COURTESY OF FERM LIVING

Interior Designer
FERM LIVING

AGE

CRAFT

Furniture with an aged patina.

Handmade tiles and artisanal finishes.

Photographer NIKOLE RAMSAY

Photographer STEPHEN KENT JOHNSON

Interior Designer
KATE BEADLE INTERIOR DESIGN

Interior Designer
COMMUNE DESIGN

TRANSITION

OPEN AIR

Linking indoor and outdoor spaces.

Outdoor shower, lounge and fire pit.

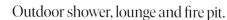

Photographer STEPHEN KENT JOHNSON

Photographer BRIGID ARNOTT

Interior Designer
COMMUNE DESIGN

Interior Designer
BRIONY FITZGERALD DESIGN

SPINNAKERS FORM A KALEIDOSCOPE ON THE WATER. BILLOWING
POPS OF LIME, PINK, AQUA AND ORANGE AGAINST DEEP BLUE.
THE SUN OVERHEAD SHARPENS THE LIGHT – IT'S A PERFECT DAY.

Photographer COURTESY OF SKAGERAK

Nautical. For lovers of this style, the beach isn't just a view to admire from afar, it's nature's playground. You adore swimming in the water, sailing, paddle boarding, surfing or running along the sand. Your home should reflect the vitality and energy that the beach gives you. It's the most active of the beach styles.

The Nautical look is fresh, clean and full of natural light. Large windows slide open to bring the outdoors in, along with the salty sea air. Bold accent colours feature against a white backdrop to give the space a lively feeling. Bright blue for the colour of the sea, red for the colour of the beach umbrella and yellow for the colour of beach sand.

This home is welcoming and inviting, ready for friends to drop in after a day of sailing or beaching. The brightly coloured door is always open and the space is unpretentious and warm – guests feel instantly at ease. The atmosphere is lively and parties are known to carry on well into the night.

NAUTICAL

NAUTICAL STYLE CUES

The Breton stripe. Seen in umbrellas, upholstery and floor rugs, it's an eye-catching staple of the Nautical beach look.

Bright beach colours used in a sophisticated way against white walls. Think blues and greens with a yellow accent.

Saturated colours. Hues are stronger and more intense, creating a fresh, upbeat atmosphere.

Sand rooms to store towels, surfboards and wetsuits. Create a hangout space by adding some speakers and a bar.

Subtle maritime references. Use rope in decor pieces or add a vintage seascape painting. Avoid contrived elements, like wooden boat wheels or wall-mounted lifebuoys.

FOUNDATION

The Nautical home needs to stand up to a busy life. When the surf's up, there's no time to worry about being too precious around the home. The space is practical but with a sense of play. It's an expression of the people who live there, but they don't take things too seriously.

The base materials need to be robust and low maintenance. Concrete is often the preferred finish for floors and can also be applied to kitchen benchtops. Floor tiles are an opportunity to introduce colour and pattern, while timber beams clad the ceiling and add warmth. White walls provide a crisp backdrop to clean, fresh colours.

Colour, and especially colour blocking, is used to create a dynamic space. Choose an impactful colour, like blue, across the walls or splashed across the floor to create an encompassing feeling. Colour blocking works well to create a cohesive, uniform look, rather than lots of small dashes of colour throughout the space, which can feel disconnected and disjointed. Consider using wallpaper such as natural seagrass for texture or an oversize wall mural. It's about bringing the feeling of the water inside and capturing the beach essence in a symbolic way.

With its optimistic, forward-thinking design, mid-century architecture complements this interior. Its forms are fuss free and spaces are open and light, matching the Nautical lifestyle perfectly.

IT LIST

Ashe Leandro – New York

Bestor Architecture – California

Bureaux – South Africa

Commune Design – Los Angeles

Hommeboys – California

India Mahdavi – France

Kennedy Nolan – Melbourne

Photographer TESS KELLY

Interior Designer
SISÄLLÄ STUDIO

This is a cosy space to retreat when it's raining at the beach, but that doesn't mean you can't get those beach vibes at home.

TIP Drench the walls and ceiling in a single colour to create an enveloping, immersive feeling.

Photographer RORY GARDINER

Interior Designer
PANDOLFINI
ARCHITECTS

An outdoor living area with built-in seating is always ready for friends. A cheerful blue-and-white stripe is a classic beach house style.

TIP   When planning, consider how you can make the most of the garden and use the space like an outdoor living area that is comfortable and shaded.

THE OUTDOOR ROOM

This is a place for ultra-relaxed outdoor living, whether chilling out in comfort or enjoying a summer evening meal with friends. The tree canopy and the stars at night provide the ceiling to your outdoor room. Trapeze lights are strung between the branches and discreetly hover over the dining space.

Living outdoors means that you fully experience the day. The sun peeping over the treetops as you're eating breakfast, al fresco style. The birds chirping as you bring your laptop outside into the cool morning air. The hot afternoon sun sees you move to a shaded patio to keep cool under a whirring outdoor fan.

Forget the kitchen; at the Nautical beach house the outdoor room is the true heart of the home. After a glorious day having fun at the beach, coming home doesn't have to mean going inside.

Cooking dinner outside is more exciting too – this provides a full outdoor kitchen that leaves the indoor kitchen gathering dust during the warmer months. It has a barbecue, naturally, for smoking, grilling, roasting or baking, and a handy outdoor sink for washing herbs gathered from pots.

The built-in bar is the perfect place to mix a drink for friends while you're preparing a meal. The fridge keeps the drinks cold, and an ice well means ice is within easy reach – just add garden-fresh mint, lemons and limes.

The outdoor kitchen needs to be low-maintenance and look smart. Source steel cupboard doors and drawer fronts in a matt black or charcoal powder coat. Porcelain slab benchtops are hardwearing and weather-proof; avoid white as the glare can be too bright and black can get too hot, so look for a warm concrete grey.

Outdoor furniture has a sense of fun. Powder-coated steel is hard-wearing and an iron-red colour adds a contrast that plays off against the outdoor greenery. Jaunty towels, bright scatter cushions and striped sun umbrellas in vivid colours feel whimsical yet timeless.

An outdoor shower is a must for washing off the beach sand, and don't forget somewhere to hang up the wetsuit and surfboard. A 'surf shack' with surfboard racks along one wall, some hooks in a cool, dry spot to hang wetsuits and a few shelves for miscellaneous outdoor equipment is the ideal all-purpose storage space.

FURNISHINGS

Deep, plush sofas provide maximum comfort for kicking back, while chic daybeds are perfect for lounging on. After a big day at the beach, who could blame you for taking a quick nap?

Furniture has clean lines and is unfussy, leaning towards practical mid-century shapes. Chairs have light frames in wood or steel to take on a breezy feeling, nothing too heavy or chunky. With fabrics, look for smart patterns or consider striped upholstery combined with tan leather.

The dining table is a perfect opportunity to inject a playful colour against a fresh white backdrop – using a coloured dining table makes a joyful statement. As it's usually the largest piece of furniture in the room, keep the rest of the space neutral and surround it with wooden chairs.

A built-in dining nook set against a window looking out to the sea is the ultimate in Nautical style. Place an elegant mid-century table at the centre of the setting and keep seating cushions relaxed and casually arranged.

A retro bar cart is a 'must have' piece of furniture that draws guests and easily sets the chilled vibe of the house.

Photographer NICOLE FRANZEN

Interior Designer
BUNSA STUDIO

A fresh dining area that's as bright and breezy as the weather outside.
Pattern has been used effectively in the banquette seating, adding a touch
of excitement to the space and giving it a casual yet elegant feel.

NAUTICAL

BEACHSIDE MODERN

Photographer NICOLE FRANZEN

Interior Designer
B&CO. BUILDERS

A board room of a completely different kind. This is more than just a storage space for your surfboards; it's a cool place to hang out. This space is clad in wood shingles and is complete with a bar. Just add a boom box and some snacks!

STYLING

The Nautical style is all about being active outdoors, so why not display it in your home? Introduce a surfboard or pair of kayak paddles for the ultimate in beach house interior styling. Use art to reference the beach: large-scale artworks such as abstract paintings or vintage posters in clean, bold colours make a vibrant statement.

Styling is relaxed and loose. The cushions aren't lined up in neat rows, they are casually tossed on the sofa, but in a chic way. Treasured travel mementos make a display alongside a well-read library. You like to get out there and have fun, so your home is not too serious or contrived. There should be something unexpected and with a sense of humour. It could be an entry foyer that features vibrantly coloured artwork or even a fish sculpture hanging above the bed!

Feature lighting can bring nautical charm to a space and the Knotty Bubbles Chain Chandelier by Lindsey Adelman Studio is perfect. The randomness of the rope that ties together the glass balls recalls a marine buoy drifting along ocean currents.

NAUTICAL PLAYLIST

'Good Vibrations' by The Beach Boys

'Hot Girl Summer' by Megan Thee Stallion ft. Nicki Minaj & Ty Dolla $ign

'Rock Lobster' by The B-52's

'Surfwax America' by Weezer

COLOUR

The colour palette for the Nautical home comes directly from a sunny day at the beach. Naturally, this includes blue and yellow inspired by the water, sky and sand, but look at the bold colours on surfboards, yachts and paddle boards.

To capture some of that vibrancy and playfulness, start with a fresh white backdrop with blue as the main colour and layer in some yellow or a warm red. Be careful not to get too carried away with all the primary colours at once, a playful space is great but avoid a kindergarten vibe!

Wood is essential to the Nautical look. Natural timber tones help soften saturated colours that can look stark against white. Rich, warm wood-panelled walls, wooden furniture or built-in joinery can provide a neutral counterpoint to the colours in the room.

The Nautical look uses colour in unexpected ways with splashes of colour on stair risers and doors. There is a sense of joyfulness in living with colour, especially when those same colours are found just outside the door. It feels lively, fresh and connected to nature.

NAUTICAL TIP: COLOUR

Bold, clean colours can bring a space to life, but don't use them everywhere at once. Choose two main hues such as blue and green, and only include a small accent in another colour, for example, yellow.

Break up the colours with materials such as wood or concrete.

Commit to colour. Using a few coloured cushions as highlights won't give that injection of life into the space; it will only look disjointed. Larger pieces, such as the sofa or dining table, in rich shades will give the space impact, creating a dynamic feel.

Photographer STEPHEN KENT JOHNSON

NAUTICAL

Interior Designer
COMMUNE DESIGN

Every corner of the house is an opportunity to create a thoughtful space layered with art, colour, texture and pattern.

TIP   White walls aren't the only neutral; a wood-panelled wall is also a perfect backdrop to layer colour and pattern.

RESOURCES

FINISHES

Consider concrete floors for robust practicality. On the walls, fresh white paint with a warm feel. Try Dulux Natural White or ask your paint store for a white with a subtle warmth. For accent colours of yellow and blue, try Dulux Happy, a bright, strong yellow that's perfect for a front door; Dulux Sky Eyes is a clean blue ideal for a living room statement or kitchen cabinetry. Look for reds in an ox-blood tone that pairs with blue in a sophisticated way, like Henna Red by Dulux.

Discover brightly patterned floor tiles in ranges from popham design tiles or Marrakech Design. If you want to use wallpaper, Acquario by Cole & Son or Poseidon by Pierre Frey are suited to a nautical theme.

FURNITURE

Go low and loungey with loose cushions for maximum comfort. For inspiration, look at sofas from Jardan and ASH NYC or vintage Vico Magistretti chairs from 1stDibs or Chairish. Try blue and white textiles with tan leather that only gets better with age.

LIGHTING

Explore character-filled lighting from Workstead or Dowel Jones, colourful PET Lamps from Spence & Lyda or lighting from Marz Designs. The Knotty Bubbles Chain Chandelier by Lindsey Adelman Studio delivers whimsy and nautical charm.

STYLING

Be inspired by vintage posters from The Galerie Fitzroy and original artworks like those by Adam Lester at Jan Murphy Gallery.

BED LINEN

Seek out soft jersey bed linen that is stretchy and forgiving like your favourite T-shirt. For inspiration, browse collections from Abode Living or Kip&Co, or visit your local linen suppliers.

HOME FRAGRANCE

Floral Street's Sunflower Pop candle has lively notes of orange with a splash of bergamot, warming white cedarwood, mint and a pop of sparkling bellini. It says beach!

01.
02.
03.
04.
05.
07.
06.

01. *Visions of Johanna,* 2017, by Adam Lester
02. Frotte Striped Bath Sheets by HAY
03. Nelson Saucer Crisscross Bubble Pendant by HAY
04. Wooden Secretary by HK Living
05. Virkelyst 3-Seater Sofa, Sea Blue Stripes by Skagerak
06. Sobremes Stripe Cookie Jar by HAY
07. Losaria Pillow in Ochre by Audo Copenhagen

Photographer HOMMEBOYS

Interior Designer
HOMMEBOYS

A shell-like wall sconce paired with a framed photo against a white wall feels
fresh and a little bit nautical.

Photographer NICOLE FRANZEN

Interior Designer
BUNSA STUDIO

Forget the mud room, the beach house has the sand room and it's the perfect place to store everything needed for fun at the beach. A row of hooks for hanging towels and hats, and each member of the family has a locker to store their shoes or flippers. Here, the patterned cement tiles add a playful touch to the timber cabinetry.

Interior Designer
DOROTHÉE DELAYE
STUDIO

A cosy bedroom in a beach house in the south-west of France contrasts complementary colours – red and green.

Photographer MR. TRIPPER

Photographer MR. TRIPPER

Interior Designer
DOROTHÉE DELAYE
STUDIO

An organised home starts at the front door. When everything has its place, you can truly relax. The built-in key-drop bench at the entry means never searching for the keys again.

Photographer STEPHEN KENT JOHNSON

Interior Designer
COMMUNE DESIGN

Not all beach houses need to have blue bathrooms! This graphic tile feels lively and bold, yet the limited colour palette of black, white and wood lends a laid-back vibe.

Photographer MR. TRIPPER

Interior Designer
DOROTHÉE DELAYE
STUDIO

A classic beach house colour combo:
yellow and blue, with a modern take.
A wavy bedhead with a built-in light
is a clever use of space.

TIP   When using yellow on the walls,
there should be a good amount of
grey tint so that it leans towards
a mustard rather than acid yellow..

HOMMAGE
AU SURF
La Première Exposition
Française de Surf

3 au 8 Aout   Galerie Biarritz   1989

TOUS LES JOURS De 10 A 18 HEURES, DIMANCHES & FÊTES EXC.

Photographer MR. TRIPPER

Interior Designer
DOROTHÉE DELAYE
STUDIO

This beach house achieves a laid-back, stylish ambience by mixing natural materials such as wood and rattan with saturated colour.

TIP   A built-in desk means that the corner of this room is used most efficiently.

Photographer MR. TRIPPER

Interior Designer
DOROTHÉE DELAYE
STUDIO

A lesson in using line and colour with restraint. The wallpaper lends a tailored look against the handmade nature of the Zellige wall tiles.

TIP   Learning about the elements and principles of design and choosing to employ one or two in a space will yield a strong, cohesive result.

Photographer: MR. TRIPPER

Interior Designer
DOROTHÉE DELAYE
STUDIO

This is luxury, undone. The marble elevates the bathroom, yet it doesn't feel stuffy or uptight. The whimsical rattan wall light adds humour.

TIP Bathrooms can be decorative when you choose an unexpected wall light and a complementary patterned fabric for the window furnishings.

Photographer MR. TRIPPER

Interior Designer
DOROTHÉE DELAYE
STUDIO

A wonderfully stylish yet laid-back space with a bold use of colour in the draperies against a white backdrop.

Photographer STEPHEN KENT JOHNSON

Interior Designer
COMMUNE DESIGN

This beach house in Santa Cruz perfectly captures the bohemian surf culture of the area. Locally milled Monterey cyprus is used internally and externally, which strongly connects the home to the local area.

Photographer STEPHEN KENT JOHNSON

Interior Designer
COMMUNE DESIGN

The focus is on the expansive view of Monterey Bay, California. The open tread
of the staircase allows for transparency and maximum enjoyment of the view
while natural light streams into the space.

Photographer STEPHEN KENT JOHNSON

Interior Designer
COMMUNE DESIGN

A thoughtful zone that caters to every need: a window for fresh, beachy air beside a plush bench seat with a handy overhead light, books and cosy wood panelling. A practical space, and one that feeds the soul.

Photographer STEPHEN KENT JOHNSON

Interior Designer
COMMUNE DESIGN

With a table and chairs by George Nakashima Woodworkers, the main bedroom is perfectly proportioned for a quick morning coffee before the rest of the house wakes up.

TIP   When you think about how you want to live, right down to your daily routine, you can home in on how each space should function uniquely to your needs.

Photographer STEPHEN KENT JOHNSON

Interior Designer
COMMUNE DESIGN

Artwork can be so much more than a painting. This textile piece by Kira Dominguez Hultgren was commissioned by the clients and includes fabric remnants from the clothes they wore on their first date. What a beautiful touch!

NAUTICAL

Interior Designer
BUNSA STUDIO

This wood-panelled bedroom is reminiscent of the craftsmanship seen in luxury yachts. Inspired by the New England location, Bunsa Studio tapped into the charm of coastal homes built in the area in the 1930s, without defaulting to cliches.

Interior Designer
COMMUNE DESIGN

A wonderfully warm, expressive and homely kitchen. Using just three materials –
Monterey cypress, soapstone for the benchtops, and plaster casing for the
rangehood – it is perfect in its simplicity.

Photographer STEPHEN KENT JOHNSON

Photographer STEPHEN KENT JOHNSON

Interior Designer
COMMUNE DESIGN

What could be better than a beach house with bunk beds? Adding a curtain to each bed! Kids and adults alike can't resist the 'cubby house' appeal of feeling totally snug by drawing the curtain.

Photographer MR. TRIPPER

Interior Designer
DOROTHÉE DELAYE
STUDIO

Wood panelling is a traditional method of cladding walls, but Dorothée Delaye Studio has interpreted this in a completely original way. The house is located at a popular surf destination in France, and this timber homage to surf culture makes perfect sense here.

NAUTICAL

Architect
FELDMAN
ARCHITECTURE

Interior Designer
COMMUNE DESIGN

Abundant surf racks are just the beginning when it comes to this surf shack.
It's complete with a bar that spills out to an interior courtyard.

Photographer STEPHEN KENT JOHNSON

FAN OVERHEAD SPINNING LAZILY AS YOU DRESS THE OUTDOOR
TABLE . GUESTS ARE ARRIVING. MORNINGS ARE FOR SWIMMING.
AFTERNOONS FOR RESTING. EVENINGS FOR FOOD AND FRIENDS.
SUMMER DAYS HAVE A HAZY PATTERN ALL OF THEIR OWN.

Photographer COURTESY OF FERM LIVING

If you love nothing more than being at the beach surrounded by sea and sand, the chances are you want to feel the beauty of nature at home too. After a gorgeous day in the sun at the beach, it's a pleasure to come home to a relaxing space where you can put your feet up and chill. To keep that relaxed feeling going, the Natural home needs to be practical, comfortable and effortless.

Natural spaces can look beautiful but they're not precious; there's a sprinkling of sand on the stone floor and the dog is sprawled on the sofa, but that's fine. These are spaces for living in. The rooms have a crafted feel; we can see that pieces have been handmade and feel their energy. Buying from local makers adds to the hewn feel of the space.

There's a focus on enjoyment, but also on healthy living spaces and a clean environment. Paints and other finishes are chosen for their low volatile organic compounds, meaning the air is as pure as you can make it.

The vibe here is casual and laid-back, but nothing about this look has happened by accident. The secret to an intentional yet casual look lies in editing; every choice is considered, and what is left out of the space is just as important as what is there.

NATURAL

NATURAL STYLE CUES

Feel close to nature with hard-wearing, natural materials like wood, rattan, leather, linen, wool and stone.

Practice wabi-sabi – find beauty in imperfections. The crack in the grain of wood and the softness of worn leather only makes them more beautiful.

Embrace a relaxed approach to design, knowing that no two pieces of wood, steel or stone will ever be identical.

Avoid printed, coloured and manufactured textiles; instead, use undyed or naturally dyed fibres.

Use textures and surfaces that show a worn patina; stone is unpolished, with a leathery, honed feel. Timber floors have a brushed texture with no shine.

Combine vintage pieces for that element of the unexpected. Not only is it more sustainable, giving new life to pre-loved objects, it provides a unique look.

FOUNDATION

Natural architecture blurs the line between the interior and outdoors. Living areas extend outside if the weather permits. But even when it's not practical to be outside, this style encourages that outdoor feeling – inside. Large sliding doors open to an outdoor living room complete with sun loungers and outdoor sofas. Natural light floods the space through large windows and skylights.

And if your home doesn't have an outdoor living space? You can still create a relaxed beach style. Bring potted trees inside, or use large windows to visually extend the living areas. Borrow views from beyond your own garden. It could be a distant view, treetops over the neighbour's fence or an upward view of the sky and clouds. This concept is not new; it's the traditional East Asian concept of *shakkei*, which translates to 'borrowed landscape' or 'borrowed scenery'. By framing views, you can facilitate a greater connection between your home and the surrounding views.

The interiors here are neutral with wood or stone floors, not forgetting the ceiling with rustic wooden beams or ceilings clad in timber. The base of the interior is subtle with a focus on texture rather than colour.

IT LIST

Amber Interiors – California

Claire Cousins Architects – Melbourne

Georgina Jeffries – Melbourne

Sarah Sherman Samuel – West Michigan

Sarah Solis Design Studio – California

Photographer MILLY MEAD

NATURAL

Architect
ANDREW BURGES
ARCHITECTS

Interior Designer
DAVID HARRISON AND
KAREN McCARTNEY

The key to creating a lively neutral space in whites, creams and natural wood tones is texture. Contrasting textures – the smooth concrete floors and rough textured brick teamed with wool upholstery and woven rattan – make this space sing.

Photographer NICOLE FRANZEN

Interior Designer
BUNSA STUDIO

The clean lines of this outdoor dining setting provide restful sophistication. Overhead, lanterns light up in the evening. Structural boughs and lush garden greenery form a striking backdrop.

TIP   Although teak is a hardwearing timber suited to outdoor furniture, it does require some general maintenance. To preserve its original honey-golden colour, use a suitable furniture oil on a regular basis.

THE OUTDOOR ROOM

The Natural outdoor room is practical, but with a touch of romance. The look is effortless with natural materials, timber or rattan chairs, comfortable sofas and cushions in neutral outdoor fabrics of white, beige or putty. It's laid-back and chic. The focus is on simplicity and getting back to nature.

A dining table and chairs in wood that is slightly greyed off and smooth, showing evidence of dinner parties over many summers. A simple yet comfortable wooden sun lounger paired with a smart white umbrella and cushion provides stylish comfort with minimum fuss.

After returning from a leisurely day at the beach, covered in sand, it's a priority to rinse off, but more than that, you want to rejuvenate your body and refresh your mind. Create an outdoor shower that's more than a shower rose attached to a wall outside –make it an immersive experience.

A transitional indoor/outdoor bathing design lets you rinse off under an outdoor shower, then walk inside to bathe. Evoke a soothing spa vibe with exotic scented oils and chilled-out music. An outdoor deck with a large sliding door leading directly into the bathroom is ideal. And as you're getting ready for the day, you can open the sliding glass door to the elements and let the fresh morning air wake you up.

Alternatively, consider creating an outdoor bathing space to complement the outdoor room: a timber deck with drainage hidden underneath, a fully plumbed Japanese wooden bath – perfect for soaking in steaming aromatic water while surrounded by nature – and a wooden slatted screen for privacy.

FURNISHINGS

Leave those uptight, overstuffed sofas at the door; the Natural look aims for maximum comfort with low-slung, lazy sofas. The sink-in kind of sofa with a deep seat that makes it hard to do anything but relax. For the ultimate casual beach look, consider a hanging basket chair or even a hammock inside so that you can enjoy that summer feeling all year round. Yes, inside!

Source a characterful vintage piece to make a statement – if everything is too neutral the space can look flat and dull. For that unexpected element, hunt down an armchair from the 1970s and reupholster it in a nubby, textured boucle fabric or slubby linen upholstery fabric – then throw over a sheepskin.

Dining tables made from wood slabs should show a live edge. That way, the raw, unique character of the tree is experienced each time you dine, bringing nature indoors. Balance the rustic nature of this dining table with a refined chair in wood with rattan or fabric upholstery.

NATURAL TIP: TEXTURE

Keep this space serene and calm by restricting the colour palette to white and the colours inherent in natural materials. Texture is the main element for this look.

Textures need to contrast – think soft linen curtains pooling on a cool concrete floor or the woven rattan of a chair on a shaggy wool rug. Use contrasting textures to achieve a detailed, comfortable look. A mix of textures creates interest when the colours are similar.

Where your home has plain white walls and few architectural features, consider a handmade jute wall hanging and an indoor plant. They add instant texture and warmth to any space.

Photographer TIMOTHY KAYE

Architect
SIMON COUCHMAN
ARCHITECTS

Interior Designer
SIMONE HAAG

The pieces in this arrangement speak to each other; the vases, lamp and cork stool all share rounded, organic forms. They sit together to create a warm and chic seating area.

TIP Go low when you want to relax to the max! Low sofa seating recalls 1970s loungey vibes, creating a laid-back mood.

Photographer NICOLE FRANZEN

Architect
THOMAS MELHORN

Interior Designer
BETSY BROWN

A statement entry sets the scene for this house. A monolithic wooden table exudes a grounded, permanent feeling. An abstract artwork gives an edginess to the space.

TIP   Contrast rustic furniture with something fresh and smooth, like this crisp white plaster wall. For a chic look, avoid layering too many rustic textures.

STYLING

With a neutral base for the interior, the styling is even more important. To keep this space from looking flat, inject interest and personality with some thoughtful decor pieces.

Pair ceramic vessels that have a coarse aged finish – the look of ancient ceramic ruins – with handmade baskets. On the floor, layer rugs in soft irregular patterns woven in unbleached wool and use cushions in plush boucle fabric.

Wherever possible, purchase pieces ethically made by artisans, rather than mass-produced in a factory. These crafted pieces have an individuality and unique quality that can only be produced through the authenticity of human hands.

The look is down-to-earth and unfussy but considered. An entry area should greet you with a warm welcome yet also be practical. Hang woven baskets and hats alongside rustic seaside decor pieces on wooden hooks. Put the kids' plastic goggles and colourful everyday paraphernalia inside one of the baskets rather than on display, to keep the look intentional.

Add instant freshness with some large leafy branches displayed simply in a vase on top of a rustic wood slab table. A classic urn lamp beside a dish to house the keys, with an artwork in neutral tones to complete the scene. The focus is on texture rather than colour.

Artwork isn't the hero in Natural beach houses, where the mood is more pared back. Instead of a show-stopping painting consider something that blends into the space, like a three-dimensional form. Look for a seagrass wall hanging, a driftwood piece or macrame to make a strong textural statement.

COLOUR

The aim is to create calm, serene spaces and this calls for a tonal approach with less focus on contrasting colours. Instead, the colours used are those found in natural materials such as undyed wool, raw stone and wood. Add bursts of colour using foliage. This colour palette is smooth and peaceful, comprising cream, beige, cinnamon, cognac, coffee, tobacco, terracotta and tan.

These natural materials can be set against a clean white wall that elevates them and gives an airy, fresh feeling. Or use a beige textured wall finish to create an earthy, cosy atmosphere. Give thought to how you want the space to feel: fresh and bright versus cosy and warm.

In between white and beige is a whole world of whites. Look for warm whites that lean into creamy tones rather than cool whites with a blue-grey hue. It's worth testing out different whites by painting up some A2-sized boards and moving them around in the space. That way you're able to see how they behave in varying light, in the corners of the room and at different times of day.

For a metallic accent, use brass, but make sure it's unlacquered so that you can watch it age gracefully.

NATURAL PLAYLIST

'Chateau' by Angus & Julia Stone

'Everybody Loves the Sunshine' by Seu Jorge and Almaz

'Myth' by Beach House

'So Good at Being in Trouble' by Unknown Mortal Orchestra

Photographer HOMMEBOYS

Interior Designer
HOMMEBOYS

This kitchen takes a casual approach with glass cupboards to effortlessly display kitchen items. It's a working kitchen after all, so no need to hide everything away.

TIP Don't neglect to decorate the kitchen; use floor rugs and vases to connect it to the other living areas.

NATURAL

RESOURCES

FINISHES

On the floors, use wide oak boards or unfilled travertine stone. On walls, try a Venetian plaster finish in putty, white or beige. The right shade of white paint is one that provides a warm undertone. Ask at your paint store or try Buff It by Dulux.

FURNITURE

Search for vintage pieces from your local auction house or go online through 1stDibs or Chairish. Seek out handmade Moroccan *Beni* rugs. The Dreamer Couch by Pop & Scott Workshop, Bobby Bar Stool by DesignByThem or the Togo Settee by Ligne Roset will enhance that casual feel. Explore pieces by furniture designer and stylist Sarah Ellison.

LIGHTING

Think pendant lights in woven raffia or rattan or, for an oversized option, see the striking STRIKHA by FAINA. More inspiration can be seen in the Lamp de Marseille by Nemo Lighting and the rattan Issa Wall Sconce by Mitzi.

STYLING

Aged ceramic vessels in natural-coloured glazes from your local thrift store or pottery studio; tuck in a primitive wooden milking stool. Or look for handcrafted slouchy baskets or wall hangings from The Dharma Door.

BED LINEN

Layer a slubby woollen throw rug over natural linen. The best part of this intentionally relaxed look – no ironing required!

HOME FRAGRANCE

Seaweed, sage, sea salt, ambrette and grapefruit create an organic beachy sensibility. Try the Wood Sage & Sea Salt Home Candle from Jo Malone.

01.
02.
04.
07.
03.
05.
06.

01. Roly Poly Chair by Faye Toogood (Image by Ludovic Balay)
02. Wicker Lamp Pendant by HK Living
03. Athens Rug by Ferm Living
04. F Chair Outdoor by GUBI
05. Dou Floor Lamp by Ferm Living
06. Dodu Pot Tall and Low by Ferm Living
07. Piscina Side Table by SARAH ELLISON

Photographer HOMMEBOYS

Interior Designer
HOMMEBOYS

An oversized pendant with an organic shape adds a sense of drama to this serene dining area. Here, the focus is on natural tones of wood, leather and wool that harmonise perfectly against a fresh white backdrop.

Photographer HOMMEBOYS

Interior Designer
FLORES TEXTILE
STUDIO

Window furnishings are key to softening the architecture and the rustic wood finish. Here, voluminous white sheer drapes filter the light and conjure a dreamy quality. The natural tones and organic shapes help connect the room back to nature.

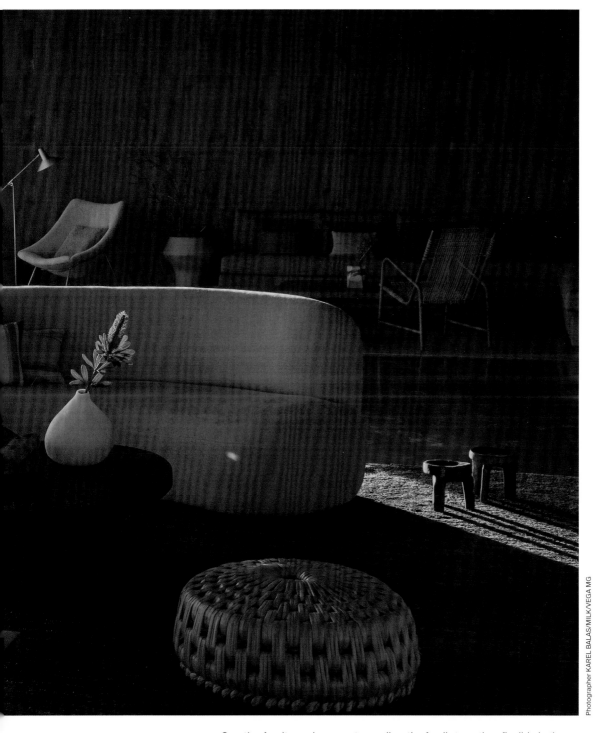

Photographer KAREL BALAS/MILK/VEGA MG

TIP   Creative furniture placement can allow the family to gather, flexibly, in the same space. This room has two zones: a quiet, streamlined area set against the back wall; and a convivial 'island' with sofa in the middle of the space, anchored with a rug for a chic arrangement of side tables, lamp and armchair.

NATURAL

Interior Designer
FLORES TEXTILE
STUDIO

It's not all about the look; it's also how the space feels. A cool breeze ruffles sheer drapes, bringing relief after a hot summer's day. Dinner is cooking and there's a scent of fresh lemon being squeezed. This dining area provides the perfect backdrop to memorable summer dinners.

Photographer KAREL BALAS/MILK/VEGA MG

Photographer KAREL BALAS/MILK/VEGA MG

Interior Designer
FLORES TEXTILE
STUDIO

This space blends indoor and outdoor bathing. The organic shape of the bath echoes the natural shape of a shell. From the deep tub there are the views and scents of the garden. A linen curtain offers privacy and softens the hard surfaces of the bathroom.

Photographer NICOLE FRANZEN

Interior Designer
B&CO. BUILDERS

This bathroom offers the best of both worlds. The shower has a sliding door that opens to an outdoor shower so you can rinse off the sand before going inside.

TIP When designing a beachside bathroom, look for practical solutions. A slatted screen provides privacy in this indoor/outdoor bathroom.

NATURAL

Architect
THOMAS MELHORN

Interior Designer
BETSY BROWN

The soft greys of the surf and beiges of the sand at Jupiter Island, Florida, unite to create a peaceful, harmonious living area. The raw oak wood floors, natural linens and limed cypress were chosen to respect the setting. This space perfectly captures the airiness of a still day at the beach.

Photographer NICOLE FRANZEN

Photographer ANSON SMART

Architect
TOBIAS PARTNERS

Styled by
CLAIRE DELMAR

Edra's On the Rocks sofa is irregular in shape and encourages some serious lounging. At the same time, it works as a soft sculpture in the space.

TIP   Sofas in an entertaining space need to be comfortable for sitting rather than sprawling. A shape-shifting sectional sofa like this one lets you get creative.

Photographer ANSON SMART

NATURAL

Architect
TOBIAS PARTNERS

Styled by
CLAIRE DELMAR

This Sydney beach house has framed window views of lush treetops. The windows slide open and the feeling of expansiveness is heightened without a corner window support.

TIP   Not all windows need to be floor to ceiling. An intentionally framed view can offer privacy from outside without the need to cover up windows completely with curtains.

Interior Designer
FERM LIVING

The vibe is laid-back and effortless. No time to be arranging seven pillows on the bed ever-so-perfectly. There's nothing try-hard about this styling; it's a casual but considered approach.

TIP   A tonal colour palette brings a room together. The contrasting textures make the room sing with slubby linen, jute rugs on cool terrazzo floors and soft sheer curtains.

Photographer COURTESY OF FERM LIVING

90

BEACHSIDE MODERN

Photographer HOMMEBOYS

Interior Designer
HOMMEBOYS

Natural materials needn't be predictable. This charming bobbin-style wooden armchair is full of character. The patterned rug provides just enough visual interest to the room against the stunning views of Northern California.

Photographer MILLY MEAD

Architect
ANDREW BURGES
ARCHITECTS

Interior Designer
DAVID HARRISON AND
KAREN MᶜCARTNEY

A sweet corner of a bedroom in Bondi. The artwork perfectly pairs with the texture of the wall and colours in the bed linen for a harmonious outcome.

TIP A wall light frees up the bedside table but be careful not to mount it too high. The aim is for adequate reading light, not feeling like you're under the spotlight.

Photographer BRIGID ARNOTT

92

Interior Designer
BRIONY FITZGERALD
DESIGN

Fresh and chic. Light streams down the staircase and through white battened partitions. The white backdrop highlights the beauty of the natural wood table and chairs.

TIP   V-groove or shiplap wall cladding will instantly lend a beachy vibe. Keep the look contemporary with a fresh white paint – try Dulux Natural White or Vivid White.

Photographer BRIGID ARNOTT

Interior Designer
BRIONY FITZGERALD
DESIGN

A hallway need not be dull. This warm timber-clad passage is both interesting and practical with storage space for hats and bags.

TIP In a circulation space, careful editing is key. For a stylish look, display an eclectic array of items in neutral materials and tones.

Architect
ANDREW BURGES
ARCHITECTS

Interior Designer
DAVID HARRISON AND
KAREN MᶜCARTNEY

The outdoor courtyard becomes a part of the interior space. It's no surprise to learn that this house is owned by William Dangar, one of Australia's pre-eminent landscape designers.

TIP An internal courtyard makes interior spaces feel expansive and light-filled. The feeling of connection to the outdoors is worth the sacrifice of space.

Photographer MILLY MEAD

A KING TIDE HAS WASHED THE BEACH, REVEALING WATERY DINOSAUR FOOTPRINTS IN ANCIENT ROCKS. DOGS TRIP BETWEEN THE MINIATURE POOLS, IGNORING THE RAIN. THE HOME FIRE IS CALLING BUT WINTER BEACH WALKING IS ADDICTIVE.

Photographer JONAS BJERRE-POULSEN

There's more to enjoy at the beach than just those idyllic, bright, sunny days. There's a year of seasons and – whether cloudy, stormy, sunny or windy – they each hold their own kind of beauty.

A brisk walk along the beach when the sky is stormy and the waves are churning is a secret delight. There's not another soul for miles. The intensity of the weather focuses the senses: the crisp air as you breathe, the sound of the waves filling your ears. When you get to the clifftop, there are dark clouds moving on the horizon – time to head home and get the fire going. The beach in winter is breathtaking and invigorating and you like to bring a bit of that moody drama into your own home.

The Winter home reflects the rugged beauty of the beach. Stone-clad walls echo the texture of rocky cliff faces, rammed earth walls repeat the sandy shore, and dark furnishings reflect the storm clouds rolling over water.

The openness of the beach is captured in the spaces: how they flow, the sightlines and the way the light falls. The colours and textures of the beach are here – natural, moody and atmospheric.

WINTER

WINTER STYLE CUES

Use nature's colour palette of stormy sky over sea. Hues range from light grey to black, with a touch of dark blue.

Create a sense of drama with black accents throughout.

Materials are raw and honest and stand up to salty air. Concrete, brick, stone and steel create a luxurious undertone.

Control of natural light is key to the winter look. A shaded room feels cooler on the hottest day and cosy in winter too.

Texture is hero, especially with the restrained winter colour palette. Contrast rugged stone against smooth wood, or soft rattan against raw concrete. The tension between the cool and warm, soft and rough provides visual interest.

FOUNDATION

The Winter look is all about capturing the moody atmosphere of a beach storm. Architecture is inspired by the raw feel of the Brutalist movement. Materials such as Besser blocks, brick, concrete and stone are used for both internal and structural walls. As timeless and robust as beach cliffs, they shape the house like a monolithic structure emerging from the sand.

Storm clouds show the perfect tones of grey to translate onto walls, using a Venetian plaster finish. The volcanic sands of the beach inspire a raw concrete floor with characterful aggregate. Steel is used for contrast and in functional areas. Timber works as an accent against the cooler palette when used selectively in ceiling panelling, joinery and furniture.

The Winter home manages light carefully, so spaces are not flooded with bright light all the time. Illumination is used to create an intentionally moody atmosphere.

Windows are strategically placed to frame views and allow for greater light control. Window dressings are simple, sheer linen curtains.

A fireplace creates both visual and physical warmth in the Winter house. For a streamlined look, choose a contemporary fireplace rather than a traditional mantel and surround. This way, the fireplace is seamless and blends into the space, leaving the fire as the focal point. The look is simple: a fireplace set into a concrete or stone wall with as little ornamentation as possible.

In this space belongings are hidden from view, so storage is important. Use hallway cupboards to store everything from coats and wet-weather gear to linen and tableware. Everyday items can be concealed behind clever sliding doors to maintain a clean, open look.

Photographer JONAS BJERRE-POULSEN

Interior Designer
NORM ARCHITECTS

This house sits in a secluded coastal corner of Denmark. The living space is minimal, yet the layering of rich materials makes it feel inviting. The sofa by Italian brand Living suits the straight lines of the room and provides softness at the same time.

Photographer SIMON WILSON

Interior Designer
FEARON HAY
ARCHITECTS

This outdoor fireplace is a more
sophisticated solution than a firepit.
A chimney ensures that even in windy
weather, you can grab a blanket and
marshmallows and enjoy a fire outside.

TIP   Keep the neighbours happy
and use an outdoor fireplace with
a chimney that directs the smoke up
and away, rather than into their yard.

THE OUTDOOR ROOM

The nights might not be warm and balmy, but this doesn't mean that we can't immerse ourselves in the outdoors. With a warming fire at its heart, the Winter outdoor space operates all year round. Strategically placed walls shield the wind, and a central fireplace offers warmth; it feels cosy and protected with a starry night sky instead of a ceiling.

Large wood-battened walls can slide across a deck to provide weather protection and open again to enjoy the views. Slide them shut to create an atmosphere of privacy and enclosure.

Brick and stone courtyards with built-in bench seats layered with Icelandic sheepskin rugs and soft cushions provide perfect warmth and comfort by the fire.

A roaring fire in a fire-pit is guaranteed to draw in friends and family as they pull up chairs and wrap a woollen throw around their shoulders. It's only a matter of time before someone feels compelled to bring out the guitar.

The materials palette for the courtyard may be brick, stone and concrete, however, it's layered with plants and decor that warms it up and makes it feel inviting. Slubby wool throw blankets and cushions add comfort and are at the ready stored in large woven baskets. Portable lamps are dotted around the courtyard, hanging from branches, sitting on tabletops for dinner and lighting the pathway.

This look suits a simple, slightly sombre mood expressed in darker coloured powder-coated steel chairs and chunky wood furniture. For a touch of luxury, consider heating the dining tabletop so that your legs stay extra warm.

FURNISHINGS

Comfort is key with this look. Sofas are an irresistible place to retreat when the weather is wild outside. Look for sofas upholstered in slubby linen – ideal for curling up in – and layer a plush floor rug to add a hint of luxury to the concrete floor. Avoid brightly coloured, patterned textiles and, instead, use undyed fibres of wool and linen in their natural colours. To maintain a quiet, reflective mood, keep the colours slightly muddy and desaturated.

The furniture selection here is like a winter beachscape: sparse and pared-back. Furniture and decor elements are limited, but they are perfectly complete.

Although it may seem easier to decorate with fewer pieces, it can be difficult to achieve a minimal space that doesn't feel empty. Furniture needs to be in proportion to the room and comfortably soft, yet not fussy.

As part of an edit of your furniture, consider each piece in the space, its purpose and how well it suits the neutral colour palette. Add natural materials with a rough texture such as side tables made from a solid tree trunk; the rawness of the wood creates a warm contrast to the sleek space.

Keep surfaces clear of clutter and remove superfluous items that may disturb a quiet, serene space.

WINTER PLAYLIST

'Autumn Leaves' by Chet Baker

'A Whiter Shade of Pale' by Procol Harum

'Down by the Water' by PJ Harvey

'Into My Arms' by Nick Cave and the Bad Seeds

'Red Eyes' by The War on Drugs

'Summertime Sadness' by Lana Del Rey

Photographer TIMOTHY KAYE

Architect
SIMON COUCHMAN
ARCHITECTS

Interior Designer
SIMONE HAAG

The corner of a bedroom always
needs a comfortable armchair for
a quiet retreat, and this cushiony
leather armchair looks so enticing
for sinking into.

TIP A leather armchair should
look soft and supple, not tightly
upholstered and shiny. The natural
beauty of the leather can then be
fully appreciated.

WINTER

ELEMENTAL LIVING

Vincent Van Duysen Works 2009–2018

AD
SUPER

Photographer TIMOTHY KAYE

Interior Design & Build
MANNA MADE

Building Design
BELLHAUS DESIGN
OFFICE

A few carefully curated books and objects look uncluttered on this bookshelf
set against a handmade brick wall. It looks rich and warm yet effortless.

STYLING

Artwork and decor are intentional and minimal; the focus is on creating a wide, open feeling. The Winter look is about eliminating items, not filling the space with objects. Be selective with the pieces that are on display.

Choose a single over-scale artwork to make a bold statement, rather than many small ones, and look for graphic pieces in black and white tones. The decor is edited down to allow the architecture of the space to be the hero. They can be functional as well, like a simple rattan basket for firewood.

Candles enhance the cosy 'hygge' feelings on a wintery evening, so cluster a few white pillar candles together and let the wax naturally melt into each other for a unique sculpture.

Cushions on the sofa should be there to provide ease rather than purely for decoration. Feather-filled pillows offer peak sink-in comfort.

WINTER TIP: LIGHTING

Create a textured lighting effect to further enhance the dramatic, moody interior. Use a combination of wall lights, floor and table lamps, and pendant lights to create pockets of light and instant atmosphere.

Replace downlights with track lighting that you can direct onto wall surfaces. Downlights only light the floor, which won't create any atmosphere in the space. Think about the artwork and surfaces that you want to light and work from there.

Install dimmers for all lighting. Nothing ruins the mood faster than too-bright lighting.

COLOUR

Dark, moody, dramatic, rugged, thundering clouds, furious winds and earthy scent. These are the elements that conjure the perfect colour palette for a winter mood. Take a walk along the beach, look up at the sky, down at the sand and across the water to find the gradations of white, grey, tan and black that make up this colour scheme.

For metallic finishes, use a black metal with an aged patina – in bronze through to pewter. Brass accents add an elegant touch against the raw materials.

Add some green freshness to the space with the addition of indoor trees. Again, the key is to keep the look sculptural and go for one large tree, rather than many small plants. For example, a Chinese fan palm or fiddle leaf fig will provide the scale and shape to suit.

IT LIST

Architects EAT – Melbourne

Fearon Hay Architects – New Zealand

NICOLEHOLLIS – California

Norm Architects – Denmark

Photographer SIMON WILSON

Interior Designer
FEARON HAY
ARCHITECTS

The colour isn't added, it's inherent in the material; grey concrete is warmed up with the brown tones of the wood ceiling. Natural cream linen curtains filter the winter light. The mirror reflects views and light back into the space and the shiny surface adds refinement and a touch of understated glamour.

RESOURCES

FINISHES

The look is minimal. Employ Besser blocks, brick, concrete (both pre-cast panels with tie-rod holes or board-formed concrete) for a raw finish. Stone slabs for bench-tops but with a leathered or honed matt finish, not highly polished. Select steel windows or steel shelving with some mirrored finishes to contrast against the rough textures. Timber is used as a secondary material for ceiling cladding or chunky joinery. For the perfect black, one that isn't leaning to purple or not intense enough, try Marais by Dulux; use a Venetian plaster for a soft grey effect. For a flat grey, try Dulux Mount Buller.

FURNITURE

Comfort is key. For boxy, soft sofas with linen upholstery try the NeoWall sofa, designed by Piero Lissoni, from Living Divani. For contrast, see the steel frame of the Officina dining chair by Magis, the classic Flag Halyard armchair by PP Møbler or the luxe look of Little Petra by &Tradition.

LIGHTING

There's a world of lighting to set the mood in the Winter house with inspiration from Multi-Lite pendant by GUBI, the Lampadaire Droit floor lamp by Serge Mouille Editions and the w102 by David Chipperfield from WÄSTBERG. Pendant lighting from Golden Editions uses a traditional Ghanaian basket weaving technique.

STYLING

Consider sculptural pieces in stone and steel by South Korean artist Lee Sisan via 1stDibs and organic clay sculptures by Jan Vogelpoel. Use branches instead of fresh flowers for architectural style.

BED LINEN

Layer up inky hues of linen with a hand-spun llama throw with tasseled edges from Pampa's Puna collection. Check out wool mills or makers in your region.

HOME FRAGRANCE

Think eucalyptus, smoke, pepper, musk. For fragrance notes of smoke and fir, try the Flamingo Estate Clarity Candle.

01.

02.

03.

04.

05.

06.

07.

01.   w102 by David Chipperfield from WÄSTBERG
02.   Ceramic Vase Espresso by HK Living
03.   Marble Kitchen Board Burgundy by HK Living
04.   Abstract Wall Chart Black/White by HK Living
05   Rico Divan by Ferm Living
06.   Unity Stool by Zanat
07.   Rice Paper Floor Shade by HAY

Photographer TIMOTHY KAYE

Architect
SIMON COUCHMAN
ARCHITECTS

Interior Designer
SIMONE HAAG

A minimal palette of black, white and timber relies on interesting forms to bring the space to life; this cone-shaped pendant light is the perfect pairing with the conical base of the terrazzo table. It also provides a dining zone within the open-plan area.

Photographer TIMOTHY KAYE

Interior Design & Build
MANNA MADE

Building Design
BELLHAUS DESIGN
OFFICE

A cosy snug in which to retreat with a good book or perhaps immerse yourself in the world of film. Lined with a black-stained timber veneer, it feels warm and quiet.

Photographer JONAS BJERRE-POULSEN

Interior Designer
NORM ARCHITECTS

A series of large, framed sliding doors allow as much sun into the house as needed, especially in the cooler months. In the summer they open to the outdoors to make the most of the expansive deck area.

Photographer JONAS BJERRE-POULSEN

Interior Designer
NORM ARCHITECTS

It's a simple gesture but a powerful one. In this minimal kitchen space,
the urn is featured to allow a museum-like appreciation. We can take a moment
to appreciate its beautiful shape and notice the way the shadows fall on it
throughout the day.

Photographer TIMOTHY KAYE

Interior Design & Build
MANNA MADE

Building Design
BELLHAUS DESIGN
OFFICE

A monolithic stone island bench in the kitchen adds movement through nature's own unique patterning. The timber veneer and Marmorino lime plaster are merely a supporting act to allow the stone to be the hero in this space.

Photographer TIMOTHY KAYE

Interior Design & Build
MANNA MADE

Building Design
BELLHAUS DESIGN
OFFICE

A practical, simple and luxurious bathroom vanity. The fluid tones of the natural stone partner perfectly with the white lime plaster walls and dark timber joinery.

TIP   When designing a bathroom, consider the lighting. Overhead lighting casts a shadow, so to apply make-up or shave with ease, thoughtful lighting is essential.

Photographer JONAS BJERRE-POULSEN

Interior Designer
NORM ARCHITECTS

A place designed for hygge, the Danish concept of enjoying the small things in life. Like relaxing on this bespoke daybed and dreaming the hours away.

Photographer TIMOTHY KAYE

Interior Design & Build
MANNA MADE

Building Design
BELLHAUS DESIGN
OFFICE

Light streams in through the blinds and plays on surfaces, creating a sense of mystery in this moody bedroom. The V-groove panelled walls are painted black for a winter spin on the usual beachy white.

Interior Design & Build
MANNA MADE

Building Design
BELLHAUS DESIGN
OFFICE

This kitchen is one for the minimalists who like attention to detail and wish to keep appliances hidden. A single shelf allows for intentional curation of objects. The effect is effortless and sumptuous.

Photographer TIMOTHY KAYE

Photographer ANSON SMART

Interior Designer
ALEXANDER & CO

Styled by
CLAIRE DELMAR

A grey materials palette that is anything but dull. The veined marble opulently clads the basin, benchtop and cupboards, and the floor shakes things up with an irregular chunky mosaic pattern. The bathroom space is softened by fresh white sheers that impart a sea-foamy feeling.

Photographer ANSON SMART

Interior Designer
ALEXANDER & CO

Styled by
CLAIRE DELMAR

With views of the sea like this, you'll want to grab the opportunity to enjoy them from every room. Here, a frameless glass door gives access to the bedroom.

Photographer SIMON WILSON

Interior Designer
FEARON HAY
ARCHITECTS

What is better than soaking in a gorgeous bath? A bath with a view and a floaty breeze. This large glass door slides across and the timber cladding of the building also opens to allow for maximum immersion into the outdoors.

Photographer JONAS BJERRE-POULSEN

Interior Designer
NORM ARCHITECTS

Friluftsliv is a Scandinavian word that translates literally as 'fresh-air life' – embracing the great outdoors whatever the weather, and plunging into nature even in the cooler seasons. After a brisk beach walk, rug up and enjoy a hot chocolate in the crisp sea air.

Interior Designer
NORM ARCHITECTS

The Japanese concept of wabi-sabi appreciates beauty that is 'imperfect, impermanent, and incomplete' in nature. In this space, it meets Danish design. The styling is pared back, so every piece must be the right choice. The imperfect vessels contrast with the perfectly smooth straight lines of the kitchen, giving the eye some relief and a focal point in the space.

Photographer JONAS BJERRE-POULSEN

TIP   Balance a large volume of space with large pendants that visually fill the area, as in this kitchen and dining room.

Photographer JONAS BJERRE-POULSEN

Interior Designer
NORM ARCHITECTS

A bunk bed like no other. The ladder takes on a sculptural form on the wall and the soft upholstered exercise ball adds an element of play to the space.

TIP Consider function – in this space, it's storage and sleeping. The custom-made joinery cleverly combines these two functions, allowing for a more spacious room.

Photographer TIMOTHY KAYE

Interior Design & Build
MANNA MADE

Building Design
BELLHAUS DESIGN
OFFICE

Handmade bricks add all the interest needed for this home office. The Winter look is rich and earthy – it feels grounded and connected to nature.

WINTER

Photographer TIMOTHY KAYE

Interior Design & Build
MANNA MADE

Building Design
BELLHAUS DESIGN
OFFICE

Rich, earthy materials were chosen to reflect the colours and textures seen in this Mornington Peninsula location. Sandy hues colour the walls, dark wood tones echo the rocks and soil, with hints of tan and green found in the grasses. It's an understated luxury that comes from knowing a place.

Photographer TIMOTHY KAYE

Architect
SIMON COUCHMAN
ARCHITECTS

Interior Designer
SIMONE HAAG

Daubs of green in the artwork, books and ceramics were chosen for this built-in cabinet and shelving.

LIKE BIRDS, THERE ARE HUMANS WHO FLY NORTH – OR SOUTH, DEPENDING ON HEMISPHERE – CHASING THE SUN. BUT STYLE-SEEKERS FIND COMFORT IN THE COCOON OF RELAXED ELEGANCE THEY'VE SPUN, WHATEVER THE SEASON.

Photographer THE INGALLS

Interior Designer
KELLY WEARSTLER

The Elevated look takes beach style to the next level, with an understated grandeur and an element of the unexpected. There are beautiful pieces gathered deliberately and meticulously from around the globe. The style is refined, aspirational and thoughtful.

This look captures the hypnotic calm of a sunset, the wonder as that stunning golden orb drops silently behind a blue horizon. This home imparts the same sense of peace with its quiet elegance; there are no loud visuals to overwhelm the space. Each room has a few 'moments' that become more apparent the longer you spend time in them: it could be an armchair by a bookcase filled with objects from your travels, or the combination of a bench seat and wall lamp in a hallway. It's personal, and each piece holds meaning.

The Elevated style showcases your personal ethos and unique knack for combining high and low, new and old; furniture from the 1970s mingles with flea market finds that sit alongside contemporary pieces. What unites these seemingly disparate objects is their sophisticated edge. While this is a less beachy aesthetic, the essence of the beach is captured and these interiors feel breezy, fresh and soothing. Spending time in this tranquil space creates a feeling of contentment.

ELEVATED

ELEVATED STYLE CUES

Calm colours. Tones of black, white and cream sit effortlessly alongside the warmth of wood and stone.

A blend of finishes. Worn patinas set against fresh, clean surfaces.

Natural stone not manufactured stone. Apply a sealant every so often as this special material warrants extra care.

Original, handcrafted or authentic designer pieces. No replicas.

A vintage floor rug adds a timeless elegance alongside contemporary pieces.

Edit. Rearrange layers and pieces within the space to transform the look and make the most of special objects.

Collections. Pieces that tell an ongoing story, and remain a work in progress, with more to be added over time.

FOUNDATION

The Elevated beach house feels airy and open, like standing at the shoreline and looking out to sea. The flow of the house makes it easy to live in; sightlines connect the spaces and wide hallways allow the house to breathe.

Start with oak floors and white walls, a look that never fails. Add in steel windows that open out to a generous patio with views – perhaps of the ocean beyond – a vaulted ceiling and some feature lighting. The result is a truly beautiful living space.

Although the interior palette of materials is simple, attention needs to be paid to the details. For instance, the timber flooring should be wide boards, and the timber should be of a grade without many knots. Look for oak in a natural or bleached finish – avoid yellow and orange tones.

Natural stone adds an element of luxury to this home, and a combination of stone finishes in nature's palette will always work. For example, pairing the irregular holes and softness of travertine with limestone and setting them against warm wood tones creates materials that sing.

IT LIST

Athena Calderone – New York

Fiona Lynch Office – Melbourne

Romenek Design Studio – California

STUDIO LIFE/STYLE – California

Photographer THE INGALLS

ELEVATED

Interior Designer
ATHENA CALDERONE

This space is less about colour and all about texture, which feels elevated and refined. The soft plaster wall finish, linen sofa, wall light and artwork are in shades of white, punctuated by the rich wood tones of the furniture. The only pattern is seen in the floor rug, its graphic shapes instantly lifting the space and giving the eye some variety.

Photographer ANSON SMART

Interior Designer
ALEXANDER & CO

Styled by
CLAIRE DELMAR

Make the most of outdoor living in style. Fling open the doors from the kitchen to a chic and well-conceived outdoor dining space.

THE OUTDOOR ROOM

The Elevated outdoor room is designed to truly live in – to be present in and savour each moment. Like the interiors, every aspect of the space has been carefully considered – it is an exercise in understated luxe.

Here is an opportunity to create multiple outdoor rooms – a dining area, a lounge and quiet corners for relaxation. This space can accommodate guests at a moment's notice, giving them a five-star resort experience with every need catered for: sun loungers with coordinated towels, lounge chairs perfectly positioned to catch the last of the sun's rays, even a rooftop patio with a dining table large enough to seat everyone. As host, you love nothing more than to create an experience that transports friends and family.

Steel-framed glass doors effortlessly open out from the kitchen to an outdoor dining room that makes entertaining a breeze.

Chunky stone pavers provide the floor of an outdoor living room complete with plush outdoor sofas. Create built-in bench seats and add custom-made cushions for a comfortable way to enjoy a fire-pit surrounded by lush green planting.

Outdoor textiles need to be extremely durable, while retaining the look and feel of natural fibres. Outdoor fabrics can be as decorative as indoor fabrics; source outdoor boucle and linen-style textiles or look for acrylic fabric compositions that are hard-wearing, but remember to bring them inside to keep them dry when not in use.

The Elevated look calls for an unusual sculptural tree such as a pom pom cypress. Trees planted in oversized ancient-looking pots add a further layer of texture. This look suits a garden that is slightly more manicured than other styles.

FURNISHINGS

The Elevated base is simple yet elegant; it provides the perfect backdrop for a layer of thoughtful furnishings. They shouldn't overpower the architecture but harmonise with it. The colours in the furniture and decor create a sense of cohesion; they sit quietly in the space and create moments to be found in every corner.

The secret to this style is the combination of pieces from different eras: the clean lines of mid-century chairs with a monolithic Brutalist sideboard; the smooth finish of a 1960s moulded plastic lamp placed on a primitive carved wood table; or the painted Gustavian footstool beside an iconic 1970s sofa. Those unexpected combinations work when the colour palette is restrained. And don't shy away from items that are 'sculptural showpieces' more than practical furniture.

Make room for beauty and awe along with those comfortable pieces which are a must.

The idiosyncratic Elevated style-hunter loves to search far and wide for the right piece, but purchases are not always expensive. A visit to the local charity store might reveal a vintage stool with a perfectly worn patina, or a ceramic pot with a one-of-a-kind glaze.

Inspiration for this well-researched look is often found in international interior design magazines. And if the perfect piece can't be found, the style-hunter might just find a local fabricator to make it. This space can't be easily created by shopping at one store. It comes together gradually with objects sourced over time, from many places.

Photographer ANSON SMART

Interior Designer
ALEXANDER & CO

Styled by
CLAIRE DELMAR

This is pure beachside glamour, Sydney style. The opening from the lounge room is framed in marble; the space is high-end, yet it feels personal and lived in.

Photographer TIMOTHY KAYE

Architect
SIMON COUCHMAN
ARCHITECTS

Interior Designer
SIMONE HAAG

An oversized artwork adds impact, and the white framing allows the piece itself to stand out.

STYLING

While the aim here is a decorative layer of styling that looks easy and elegant, a good deal of work goes into this effortless look. The Elevated beach house may be pared back, but styling is the essential ingredient that takes the space to the next level. Decor pieces lean towards art and antiques, old things with a patina that show they have been used and loved in a past life.

The local high street retailer can also provide content; clever mixing of high and low styles and price points adds soul and personality. An oversized vintage clamshell found at a thrift store, say, that mingles with a refined hand-carved marble vessel. The unique pairing of a candlestick made by a local potter with an Italian Murano glass bowl – it's unexpected and dynamic.

Styling is where you can really experiment and mix things up to change the feel of the space. Rearrange furniture pieces, move artwork around, swap out blankets and cushions as the seasons and your moods change. This shapeshifting is much easier with a limited colour palette so the space transforms effortlessly.

Here, too, there's a link between indoors and out. An indoor tree, such as a rubber tree in a large pot, gives the room life, especially in the winter months. It adds just the right amount of colour to your limited palette. Create impact in the room by using large branches of foliage. Wander the garden and fill a large vase with some green branches instead of traditional flowers.

ELEVATED TIP: VINTAGE SHOPPING

When buying vintage furniture pay attention to the shape, not the colour. The fabric or finish can be changed, but the shape can't.

Do the lift test. When shopping for vintage pieces at flea markets or auction houses, see if you can lift it up. Usually, the heavier the item, the better quality it is. Look inside drawers or under tabletops for labels that might show provenance. Remember that veneer doesn't mean it's of lesser quality, some of the best pieces are made this way.

Don't hesitate. If you stumble across a piece that is the right style, size and price, buy it. It probably won't be there when you return! And if you don't end up using it, sell it on. Don't be a hoarder.

COLOUR

The controlled colour palette here is subtle and gentle on the eye, but it's also complex; the white, black, cream and timber tones are anything but basic. Finding the perfect white paint can prove a challenge with so many shades of white to choose from. Think of cool grey whites, warm creamy whites, smoky dull whites or oatmeal beige whites – there is so much variation and nuance. While some may not see any colour in this neutral backdrop, it's everywhere.

The way that light falls in the space has its own effect on colour. Bright clean whites can feel too harsh and create glare in rooms that are flooded with sunlight, so a slightly dirty, creamy white is perfect here.

You may find that a room that doesn't get much natural light – perhaps due to its orientation or smaller windows – feels drab and flat when painted white. This is the perfect opportunity to create a moody space. Painting a room dark grey or navy is a break from white airy spaces and creates an enveloping feeling.

Don't forget that a natural colour palette draws the eye outward. Stunning external views of a garden beyond, or perhaps even an ocean, provide the added palette of nature's colours.

ELEVATED PLAYLIST

'Come Away with Me'
by Norah Jones

'Coffee' by Sylvan Esso

'Django' by The Modern
Jazz Quartet

'Lisa Sawyer' by Leon Bridges

'The Girl from Ipanema'
by Astrud Gilberto

Photographer NIKOLE RAMSAY

Interior Designer
KATE BEADLE
INTERIOR DESIGN

A perfect pairing. Colour is the easiest language in which two pieces can speak to each other. However, the similar shapes of both artwork and chair mean that these pieces truly vibe together.

RESOURCES

FINISHES

Calm and restrained with wide oak floorboards, white plaster walls and windows framed in black steel. Choose marble, travertine or limestone for benchtops and wet areas. Explore timber veneer cabinetry and try burl for a luxurious texture.

FURNITURE

Each piece is carefully selected starting with a sofa, like the elegant, curved shape of the Revers Sofa by GUBI. Look at artisanal furniture from Stahl + Band. Source antique and vintage pieces from local auction houses, at Chairish or 1stDibs. For the floor, try the solid-coloured rugs, hand knotted in wool by Armadillo or a vintage Persian rug. The characterful Pièrre side table from SARAH ELLISON combines marble, rattan and walnut.

LIGHTING

Seek inspiration in feature pendant lights from Apparatus, Volker Haug Studio, Christopher Boots and Michael Anastassiades. Light sculptures, such as the Puffball pieces by Faye Toogood for Matter Made, add an unexpected element with their unusual material combination of fibreglass and aluminium.

STYLING

Ceramics are key for styling this elevated look. Search for wabi-sabi ceramics from Japan – try a vintage importer such as Kazari. The precise and considered ceramic sculptures by Jeremy Anderson instantly elevate any space. If you like organic shapes, see the outstanding works of ceramicist Zhu Ohmu.

BED LINEN

Choose bed linen in natural shades of beige, cream and brown, with a focus on contrasting textures: heavy canvas cushions against crisp white sheets. No applied pattern is needed when textural fabrics add all of the interest. Source pure linen from bedouin SOCIETE.

HOME FRAGRANCE

Seek out the clove buds, bay, ylang ylang, carnation, guaiac wood and Haiti vetiver of the Altar Candle by Byredo.

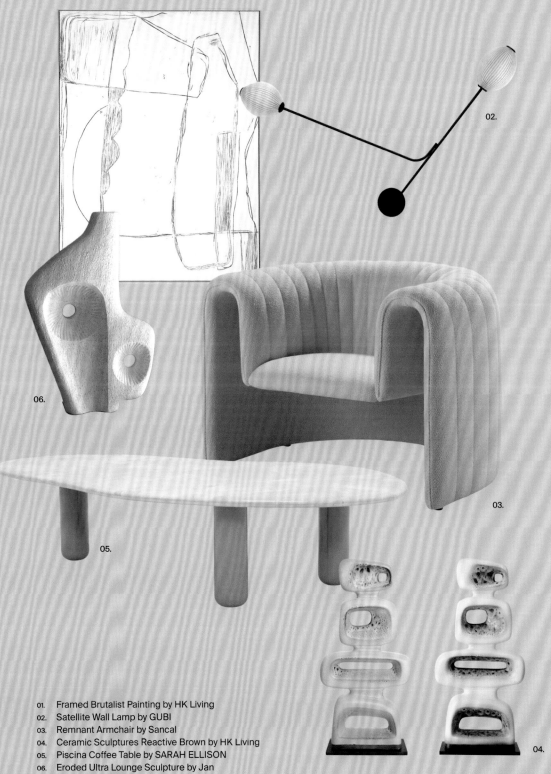

01. Framed Brutalist Painting by HK Living
02. Satellite Wall Lamp by GUBI
03. Remnant Armchair by Sancal
04. Ceramic Sculptures Reactive Brown by HK Living
05. Piscina Coffee Table by SARAH ELLISON
06. Eroded Ultra Lounge Sculpture by Jan Vogelpoel Ceramics

Photographer ANSON SMART

Interior Designer
ALEXANDER & CO

Styled by
CLAIRE DELMAR

The timber-clad ceiling creates a zone for the kitchen in this open-plan space. The American oak veneer folds down onto the kitchen cabinetry, which conceals the appliances.

TIP   Conceal appliances behind cupboard fronts so that the kitchen appears as a beautiful piece of joinery in the home, rather than a utilitarian workspace.

Photographer ANSON SMART

Interior Designer
ALEXANDER & CO

Styled by
CLAIRE DELMAR

A custom-made cabinet provides an opportunity to display ceramics and sentimental pieces sourced from near and far.

TIP Consider curating your collection of objects and edit it so there is a consistent element – it could be a colour palette, material or theme.

Interior Designer
ALEXANDER & CO

Styled by
CLAIRE DELMAR

This low modular sofa, the iconic Camaleonda by Mario Bellini for B&B Italia, beckons for a serious lounging session. The space is earthy without being rustic; warm and inviting, yet elegant.

Photographer ANSON SMART

Interior Designer
ALEXANDER & CO

Styled by
CLAIRE DELMAR

The Elevated beach house needs a statement armchair, something that is more art than chair. A piece that declares itself and brings a smile. Like this Favela Chair by the Campana Brothers – it's more a designer statement than a chair to use every day.

Photographer ANSON SMART

Interior Designer
ALEXANDER & CO

Styled by
CLAIRE DELMAR

The dining area is divided from the lounge room by a double-sided fireplace, creating a more intimate dining experience.

Photographer ANSON SMART

Interior Designer
ALEXANDER & CO

Styled by
CLAIRE DELMAR

Everyone needs a junk drawer – some just do it with elevated style! Here we see solid marble shelves for displaying special pieces, and drawers below for all the other stuff that life throws at us.

Photographer ANSON SMART

Interior Designer
ALEXANDER & CO

Styled by
CLAIRE DELMAR

A blissfully serene bedroom. There is nothing superfluous to distract the eye, it's simply a well-resolved space that feels clean and uncluttered.

TIP If you can't find a bed and nightstand combination that works for you, consider a custom design.

Photographer ANSON SMART

Interior Designer
ALEXANDER & CO

Styled by
CLAIRE DELMAR

A simple sculpture has its own moment in the corner of a room. From the hallway it draws the eye into the room, and the bold colours in the artworks connect the spaces.

TIP   Consider sightlines from a hallway and how you can artfully decorate your home. Pay attention to form and allow each object to breathe in the space.

Photographer ANSON SMART

ELEVATED

Interior Designer
ALEXANDER & CO

Styled by
CLAIRE DELMAR

This banquette seating provides a cosy nook for dining and easy conversation. The curved glass window wraps around the seating and projects into the garden. In the evening, when the round skylight isn't washing the table with sunlight, a single iconic Serge Mouille Wall Sconce provides adjustable lighting over the table. It's the perfect solution for this snug space.

Photographer NIKOLE RAMSAY

Interior Designer
KATE BEADLE
INTERIOR DESIGN

A clean white hallway with a cleverly positioned strip skylight makes for an airy, fresh entry at this coastal home in Portsea, on Victoria's Mornington Peninsula.

TIP   Rather than the default square skylights in the middle of a hallway, consider a long strip against the wall as it allows for a surface for the light to fall on, which adds a touch of drama.

Photographer NIKOLE RAMSAY

Interior Designer
KATE BEADLE
INTERIOR DESIGN

A group of rowing oars reference the beach location of this home while taking on a sculptural feel.

TIP   Be brave and take risks with what is considered 'art' for the home. Is there something that you collect? Try grouping and boldly displaying your collectibles.

Photographer NIKOLE RAMSAY

Interior Designer
KATE BEADLE
INTERIOR DESIGN

A bedroom should offer a sense of calm and security. Painting the walls in a moody grey feels enveloping and cosy.

TIP   Some bedside tables are just too small. Look at a chest of drawers instead, so that you have space for a lamp and a stylish vignette as well.

Photographer NIKOLE RAMSAY

Interior Designer
KATE BEADLE
INTERIOR DESIGN

Warm white walls awash with natural light from strip skylights provide drama here. But the hand sculpture in the bathroom beyond adds an element of humour that shows the people living here love to have fun.

Interior Designer
DOROTHÉE DELAYE
STUDIO

There's glamorous use of colour in this French beach house. The glossy green ceiling is a bold statement and gives the room a playfulness while still feeling elevated.

TIP   Painting a ceiling is not for the faint of heart but the results are well worth it. Generally, if the ceiling colour is darker than the walls, high ceilings work best, as in this room.

Photographer MR. TRIPPER

Photographer MR. TRIPPER

Interior Designer
DOROTHÉE DELAYE
STUDIO

This is a space to settle into when the surf is flat. Choose your pleasure –
the dining table for a bottomless brunch or the plush, vibrant couch for
a board game. It's cosy and lively beneath the green ceiling.

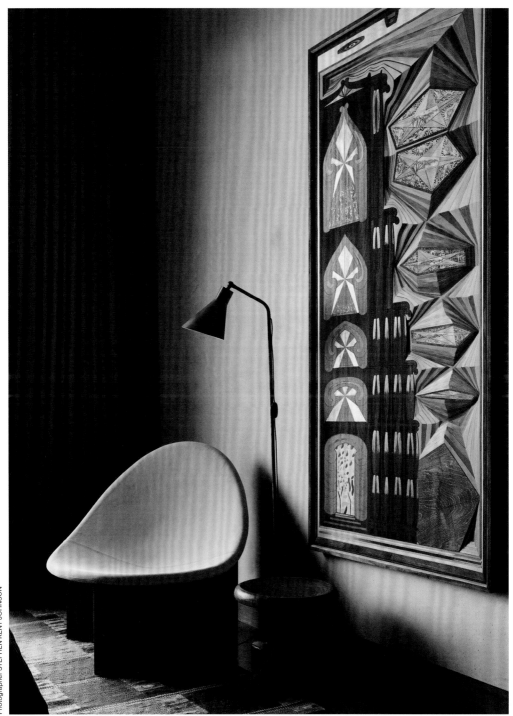

Photographer STEPHEN KENT JOHNSON

Architect
FELDMAN
ARCHITECTURE

Interior Designer
COMMUNE DESIGN

The elements of colour, form and proportion combine to create a magical bedroom corner. The curved sculptural armchair, articulated lamp and vibrant artwork sing when placed together.

ELEVATED

HERE ARE TREASURES THAT BRING JOY. A PIECE OF DRIFTWOOD
FROM WHICH TO DRAPE A GAUZY NET. A FRANGIPANI FLOWER
PICKED IN THE EARLY MORNING. THE TAIL FEATHER OF A TAWNY
BIRD – A GIFT. OPEN YOUR EYES. RICHES ABOUND.

Photographer ANSON SMART

BEACHSIDE MODERN

Interior Designer
RICHARD UNSWORTH

It's good for the soul to wander along a deserted beach picking up shells and pieces of driftwood along the way. There's satisfaction in sorting a collection of shells into neat categories – cockle shells, conch shells or even sea urchins. It's the same with the objects that you collect for your home. An afternoon spent artfully arranging treasured pieces sounds like heaven.

But there's more to the Beachcomber home than arranging pieces to make it look good; it must also feel good. And nothing feels quite as homely as being surrounded by things that have meaning. It's the Polaroid camera that belonged to your mother, the clay dishes your children made in kindergarten. When you hold these objects, memories surround you.

The Beachcomber look is collected, drawn from old things that tell a story. They bear signs of being well used and loved, like the ceramic teapot that has poured so many cups of tea. Or the dining table with knocks and dints that hint at wild parties and messy childhood meals. Life isn't perfect and nor should home be.

This space has humour and light. It's dotted about with unexpected pieces that shouldn't go together but do – like the colourful folk mask hanging alongside kitchen utensils or skateboards placed on the wall like artwork. It's these unusual juxtapositions that make the Beachcomber spaces memorable and dynamic. And there's a careful balance to maintain harmony amid the eclecticism.

BEACHCOMBER

BEACHCOMBER STYLE CUES

Layers. The look is layered with pieces collected over time. Books create an instant lived-in feel. This design isn't precious; it's about personality.

Collections. Curated to display favourite pieces, not the entire assortment at once. Rotate that set of vintage alarm clocks!

Use a gallery hang arrangement to display artwork – gather works of different sizes, styles and frames. The aim is a look that has evolved over time – it's authentic, not perfect.

On walls, try wallpaper or wood panelling – natural or painted.

Celebrate pattern. When mixing patterns ensure there is one large-scale pattern paired with a small-scale pattern so that they don't compete.

Colour. Use a key colour to connect the space and create cohesion across collections and furniture, avoiding a chaotic feel.

Surprise. Add that unexpected item that doesn't 'go' in the space. It creates tension or humour – and magic!

FOUNDATION

With the eclectic Beachcomber look, there's only one rule: express your authentic self. This approach is about the feel, over and above a perfectly stylish room.

A space that is embedded with character helps build atmosphere – so banish those cold white gallery walls. The backdrop should create the vibe. Use timber panelling to create a warm surface or paint a V-groove wall panel in a shade of green or blue, or even a warm white. The texture will add immediate interest and warmth.

Floors don't need to look pristine and perfect – it's unmistakable character that you're looking for. A wire-brushed finish on natural timber floors emphasises the grain, giving a distressed vintage look. Consider painting a plain timber floor in a solid colour, or even a checkerboard pattern. Layer with vintage Persian rugs or kilims.

BEACHCOMBER PLAYLIST

'Empty Nesters' by Toro y Moi

'Move' by Art Pepper

'Pink + White' by Frank Ocean

'Summer in the City'
by The Lovin' Spoonful

'Under the Boardwalk'
by The Drifters

Photographer ANSON SMART

Interior Designer
RICHARD UNSWORTH

There is something instinctively welcoming about this lived-in, unpretentious space where vintage furniture and art mingle. This Sydney beachfront house has charm in spades.

Photographer COURTESY OF SKAGERAK

Interior Designer
DOROTHÉE DELAYE
STUDIO

This is the sort of outdoor space where long summer days are spent with friends. It's casual and easy, with potted plants dotted about in a boho kind of way. It's a place where you can truly unwind.

THE OUTDOOR ROOM

The Beachcomber outdoor room feels lively with a festive atmosphere. There's a combination of potted plants, scatter cushions and vintage chairs that feels playful and relaxed.

It's full of character and starts with a foundation of 'crazy paved' patio space. The garden is abundant with bright flowers growing on trellises and shaded pergolas. Outdoor modular sofas heaped with scatter cushions beckon you to sprawl in the shade of an old tree. Just because it's outside doesn't mean that you can't personalise it. Put your feet up!

Vibrant glassware on a colourful cloth decorates the outdoor dining table; it sits beneath a pergola with hot pink bougainvillea flourishing overhead. Layering patterns and colours adds to the lighthearted feeling.

An outdoor lounge setting doesn't need to match, instead the look is loose and relaxed. Everyone has their own special chair to choose from – a striped sling chair, a deck chair or even a bean bag. Go with what *feels* right while keeping in mind a colour, such as blue, so that the pieces are different but coordinated. A cheerful outdoor rug ties everything together. It's laid-back and a little bohemian.

An assortment of terracotta and ceramic pots creates variety; however, choose one colour and then find pots in a variety of shapes to achieve a look that is collected yet curated. An outdoor sun mattress that you can roll up and move around the garden or take to the beach means that you can create a cosy and comfortable space anywhere.

FURNISHINGS

This look celebrates the marriage of old and new. Take a French-polished antique side table with a contemporary metal lamp on top – it's a slightly unorthodox union that works. Old pieces woven into a space give it a grounded, weighty note and this allows you to experiment with pattern and colour. The careful blending of new and old creates a balance that stops the space appearing disorganised and unruly.

A sense of history is created in a room when old things are included. They could be family heirlooms passed down, or a retro sofa from the 1970s. And while these items are not new, they can be revitalised. Consider reupholstering a tired armchair in a fabric that fits the space, or re-staining furniture to give it a whole new life.

BEACHCOMBER TIP: MIX PATTERNS

Be confident. Mixing patterns can be daunting but exciting, and immensely satisfying when you pull it off.

Make sure that there is one common colour across the patterns, with a few supporting accents. This colour will help tie the patterns together.

It's important that there is only one hero pattern, which will usually be the largest scale. If you are not sure, the fabric or wallpaper will usually have pattern repeat information.

Combine organic patterns, such as waves or floral with geometric patterns, stripes or checks. Too much of any one type of pattern will look chaotic.

Photographer STEPHEN KENT JOHNSON

Architect
FELDMAN
ARCHITECTURE

Interior Designer
COMMUNE DESIGN

A built-in bookcase can accommodate anything your heart desires. These bookshelves frame an artwork, and even accommodate a collection of guitars.

STYLING

Creating vignettes is a beachcomber's superpower. They usually have no shortage of fascinating objects to display; the challenge lies in not overdoing it. Curate collections thoughtfully – don't display the entire range at once; pare it back. Store and rotate items according to the seasons and your mood. Allow the visitor's eye to take in the many moments in the room.

Styling can change the way a space feels and looks simply by moving furniture, art and objects around the home. No construction or paintbrushes are required, but what you need is practice. Does the vintage coral sit well atop the stack of books on a rustic coffee table? Do the textures provide enough contrast? Is the scale in proportion? Use the 'rule of odd numbers' to group objects, the arrangement shouldn't look symmetrical.

A handy tip is to stand back and take a photo using your phone. The camera frames the scene and gives an objective view of the way the pieces come together.

Use unusual decor pieces to style your spaces. A beautiful instrument such as a violin can hang on the wall beside other artworks, or arrange a piece of driftwood collected from a family holiday on the coffee table. These one-of-a-kind pieces give a space meaning or atmosphere.

Group similar pieces together using a common element, such as a collection of vintage seascape paintings hanging together. It could be a common colour or material. Be mindful of scale. Too many small things in the space will look cluttered, so add an oversized artwork or large paper lantern. These larger pieces help ground the area and take up visual space.

Interior Designer
HOME BELONGING
TO ALEX McCABE

The beachcomber's home is a true expression of their tastes. This curated collection of books, albums and objects tells the story of its owners, their past and present and their future aspirations.

Photographer NICOLE FRANZEN

Interior Designer
BUNSA STUDIO

In this stylish entry, hats and bags hang neatly, shoes are stored under the bench seat and coats in cupboards. It's utilitarian but joyfully exuberant.

TIP   Unleash your decorative flair in functional areas. They can be practical and attractive when styled with expressive displays and materials.

COLOUR

The Beachcomber look is laid-back, and there are no specific rules around colour themes as it's not an overly designed style. However, to create a cosy, characterful space, we need to consider the role of colour.

The more colour in a room, the more dynamic and exciting it will be. But go too far and you risk a confused and messy look, with a muddled ambience. It's wise to select just a few colours for a space, especially when displaying treasured objects that bring their own aesthetic.

Gather some favourite pieces to see if there is a colour theme that emerges. Choosing that colour to paint the whole room will bring an instant vibe and those special pieces will sing. Add an accent colour that is slightly off-key to create unexpected excitement. It could be in a lampshade or the frame around an artwork. This is the magic of style at work.

IT LIST

Anna Spiro Design – Brisbane

Leanne Ford Interiors – Pennsylvania

Lynda Gardener – Melbourne

Reath Design – California

RESOURCES

FINISHES

Choose recycled tiles – see the range from Jatana Interiors. For painted wood-panelling, see the wide range of wall profiles in the Surround collection by Laminex. Porter's Paints has specialty finishes in a sublime range of colours – the Smooth Impasto and Interno Lime Wash are favourites.

FURNITURE

Play with family heirlooms, vintage and antique pieces; visit flea markets and auction houses or try online at 1stDibs or Chairish. For luxuriously soft, shaggy wool rugs try Beni. Consider side tables with a carved wood finish and if you don't have a local maker try the range of pieces designed by Studioilse for Zanat. Explore rattan furniture from Danish brand Sika-Design layered with a sheepskin.

LIGHTING

For an eclectic feel, choose an oversized round pendant light in taupe linen from Imprint House. Or bring some warmth into the space by hanging a pendant with sweet wicker shades such as the Issa Chandelier by Tali Roth for Mitzi Lighting.

STYLING

Add decor touches with items from treasured collections or found objects such as driftwood, shells and palm leaves. For a completely innovative take on woven wall art, see the vibrant pieces by Melbourne artist Tammy Kanat.

BED LINEN

Layer vintage quilts over crisp cotton sheets; look online at Danish store The Apartment for ideas. Kip&Co has a cheerful range that can be mixed and matched. Stripes, gingham and florals can be matched back to solid colours for a considered, eclectic look.

HOME FRAGRANCE

For an intoxicating fragrance of rose, herb garden and citrus, hunt down the Euphoria Candle by Flamingo Estate.

01.

03.

02.

04.

05.

06.

01. DORIS lamp by HK Living
02. Rico Armchair by Ferm Living
03. Bath Towel 1965 by HK Living
04. Ura Scented Candle in Red Sienna by Ferm Living
05. Touch Sideboard by Studioilse for Zanat
06. Agnes Plant Stands by Ferm Living

Photographer ANSON SMART

Interior Designer
RICHARD UNSWORTH

This comforting retreat is an oasis of calm, with its pillowy yet sleek mid-century Womb Chair. The red fabric stands on its own against the dark timber panelling.

TIP   Investment furniture can bring lasting happiness! This chair has stood the test of time; designed in 1948 it still looks fresh today.

Interior Designer
RICHARD UNSWORTH

The Beachcomber house turns the idea of matching decor on its head.
It mixes wood tones and combines furniture from different eras, and layers
of artwork are hung in a way that feels loose and spirited.

Photographer ANSON SMART

Interior Designer
RICHARD UNSWORTH

Collect the things that excite and intrigue you. They don't need to be of the same era or style or have a monetary value. A feather, some branches, a child's craft; if it carries meaning and tells a story, it's a piece worth keeping.

Photographer ANSON SMART

Interior Designer
RICHARD UNSWORTH

It's hard to tell where the garden ends and the interior begins. It all makes sense when we learn that this home is owned by Richard Unsworth, co-founder of Sydney landscape design firm and shop, Garden Life.

Photographer ANSON SMART

Interior Designer
RICHARD UNSWORTH

Boldly patterned wallpapers recall beach houses from the 1960s. You can almost hear the famous surf rock song 'Wipe Out' blaring from the record player – it's such a vibe.

TIP A bold wallpaper can feel a little less confronting when it's used sparingly in circulation spaces like hallways.

Photographer ANSON SMART

Interior Designer
RICHARD UNSWORTH

This quirky house, named Trincomalee, was built in 1896 and given a modernist bent in the late 1970s. It has been gently renovated by the latest owners who wanted to honour the house and retain its inherent charm.

Photographer ERIC ROTH

Interior Designer
NINA FARMER
INTERIORS

A 1950s beach house in Martha's Vineyard incorporates colours and textures inspired by a trip to Morocco. Nina Farmer applied tadelakt to the floors, a lime plaster finish that provides a blank canvas to layer rugs and furniture.

Photographer ERIC ROTH

Interior Designer
NINA FARMER
INTERIORS

White walls, ceiling and floor highlight
the beauty of the natural materials in
the space – the rustic wood beams,
seagrass rug and cane furniture.

TIP   A white interior need not look
cold and clinical. Be sure to layer lots
of natural textured materials to warm
up the space.

Interior Designer
BUNSA STUDIO

Books, artworks and objects gathered from travels imbue a space with unique personality. Editing and rotating collections can keep displays fresh; not everything should be on show at once.

Interior Designer
KELLY WEARSTLER

A snug library is decorated with various wall sculptures and artwork sourced from local Californian artists, adding atmosphere from the coastal Santa Monica location. Cassina Soriana armchairs are low and loungey, but the space doesn't take itself too seriously with a cheeky stool adding a sense of humour.

Photographer THE INGALLS

Photographer MR. TRIPPER

Interior Designer
DOROTHÉE DELAYE
STUDIO

The ultimate hangout. Unplug from technology; surf, skate, have a beer with friends. You don't need to be part of the surf culture to be completely immersed in this space, its charm will gently pull you in.

Photographer LEAN TIMMS

Interior Designer
SARAH ANDREWS

The Beachcomber look utilises objects that have meaning or tell a story; however, an element of cohesion is needed. This shack on the west coast of Tasmania is painted white, and the natural materials of wood and wicker sit together harmoniously.

Photographer LEAN TIMMS

Interior Designer
SARAH ANDREWS

A collection of vintage paintings that hang together in an undone, relaxed way, as though they are in conversation together.

TIP   The key to hanging artworks in a loose way is maintaining balance. They are not the same size, so hanging them in an orderly way won't work.

Photographer LEAN TIMMS

Interior Designer
SARAH ANDREWS

A bedroom should feel calm and restful, but that needn't mean boring and dull. Here, we see how a strong pattern – the stripe – is used to inject interest and life to this black and white bedroom. Above the bed hangs an unconventional light, comprising an exposed light globe with the cable wrapped around a wall hook. It's simple but distinctive.

Photographer LEAN TIMMS

Interior Designer
SARAH ANDREWS

Small elements can enrich a space by telling a story that is specific to place. A model boat, a fishing net and vintage book mingle here and spark conversation.

TIP For simplicity, choose an edited selection of objects to display. Too many disparate pieces can be visually overwhelming.

Interior Designer
SARAH ANDREWS

The landscape of western Tasmania is home to ancient rainforests, raging rivers and small quaint towns. This shack is located within a secluded slice of a world heritage area and the interiors of the space are perfectly compatible. This humble room has every necessity: a wood-burning fire, cosy dining table and a bench beside antique windows that frame views of the bay.

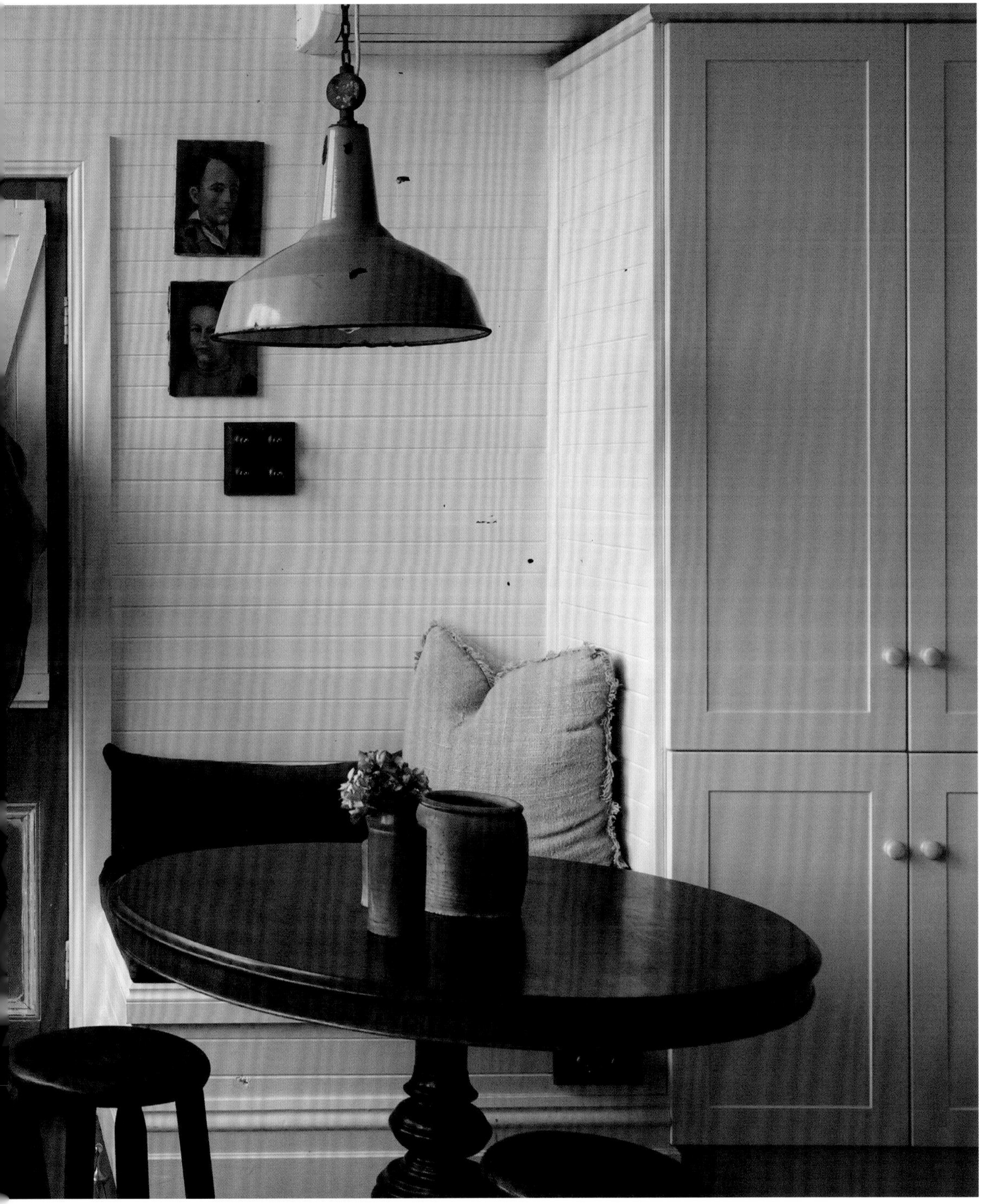

Photographer JAMES GEER

II.

Photographer NIKOLE RAMSAY

Interior Designer
KATE BEADLE INTERIOR DESIGN

DEFINING YOUR
BEACHSIDE STYLE

Beachside style is alluring, not just for its relaxed looks but also for the emotions it represents. There's a sense of freedom and escape that the beach endows us with, a simplicity and lightness to living and, for many, memories of childhood holidays or youthful liberation. Creating the 'beachside modern' style at home is a way to evoke those feelings in our everyday surrounds.

We've explored beach interiors across different regions and, by now, you may have decided which style complements your home and lifestyle. This may be driven by your location – whether in a cool climate, on a classic coastline, near inland waterways or in tropical hinterland. Perhaps you don't live near the coast but simply want to create a relaxed feel that echoes beach modern. If you're undecided, this section can help you interrogate the look that you want for your home.

First, take a small quiz to help you focus on which beach style reflects the *look* you love. It's a prompt to get you thinking about your home and the way you live, so that you can identify the style that speaks to you and your life.

Next, consider the *feel* and mood of your ideal space; it's as important as how it looks. A harmonious room that invites you to stay is the ultimate styling achievement.

Once you've identified how the space should look and feel, you're ready to begin the design process. Before you do, you'll need a *plan* to guide you as you implement your beachside look. Creating a design plan takes a little time but it ensures the results are considered and rewarding. With a plan in hand, styling decisions and selections are easier and, soon enough, you'll be a pro at shopping and editing – an essential skill to pull off a cohesive look.

As a designer, I'm continually amazed by the power of room transformations from blank canvas to beautiful, layered space. It's immensely satisfying when a room begins to come together, even more so when the result reflects your own creativity and self-expression. With a vision and a plan, you can achieve the beach house of your dreams.

BEACHSIDE MODERN

Photographer MR. TRIPPER

Interior Designer
DOROTHÉE DELAYE
STUDIO

THE LOOK

When it comes to creating your own beach look it's important to be clear on what you want to achieve, and that means understanding your preferred beach style.

When I start working with clients, I spend time learning about their everyday lives, to understand their style. It's an important, ongoing conversation that begins well before any design work commences. We discuss lifestyles, careers, families and the way they live in their homes – where they relax, how they socialise. I like to find out about clients' tastes and interests, the items they treasure that tell me a little about their past, so that I can help create an ideal home for the future.

Then I can plan the space, from renovation decisions to material finishes on walls and floors, lighting options and fabric and furniture selections through to styling. Without this important information, the result won't reflect each client's unique lifestyle.

This section of the book echoes the way I work with clients. The following questions are a fun way to start thinking about which beach style appeals to you. What other questions should you ask that might influence your style?

Use this quiz to help identify the look you want in your beach-inspired home. Take a notebook and pencil and write your very first response: a, b, c, d, e. Don't over-think it. If two answers work for you, write them both down.

1.
Your ultimate beach destination:

(a)

Greece. Its ruggedly beautiful coastline offers a taste of sailing and sunning heaven.

(b)

There's a chic shopping strip, but it's the clean, clear water that you love most at Noosa Main Beach, Australia.

(c)

The black basalt landscape of Iceland's Reynisfjara Beach with its majestic natural rock formations is awe-inspiring.

(d)

A sun lounger on the beach in Nice, France, is the place to be for beach club elegance.

(e)

Lanai island in Hawaii, hunting for a piece of history hidden in the sands of Shipwreck Beach.

2.

Your favourite piece of furniture:

(a)

That blue and white Pillow Chair by Ash NYC; it exudes relaxed glamour.

(b)

The rattan Basket lounge chair from GUBI, ever stylish since the 1960s.

(c)

A cosy shearling armchair, perfect by the fire on a chilly winter's night.

(d)

The chunky curves of the Float by SARAH ELLISON, pure 1970s nostalgia.

(e)

A retro cane armchair, one of your proudest vintage finds.

3.

You love waking up in bed linen that meets your mood:

(a)

Colourful patterned sheets for a sunny start to every day.

(b)

Calming white linen – the only colour for bedding.

(c)

Warm layers of richly hued linen with textured wool blankets.

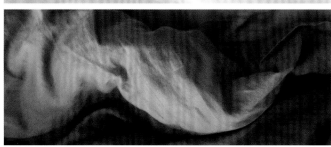

(d)

Only 100 per cent Egyptian cotton will do, luxury all the way.

(e)

Inky dark bed linen and layers of woollen throws for ultimate comfort.

4.

Your ideal day of relaxation:

(a)

With a group of friends, lazing on sun loungers under colourful parasols.

(b)

Connected to nature, laying out yoga mats for a calming session.

(c)

Staying in by the fire with design books and a glass of wine.

(d)

Styling sculptural branches into the perfect dramatic formation.

(e)

Sorting through collections, such a comforting trip down memory lane.

5.

The two colours you could live with forever:

(a)

Bright sky-blue and a punchy yellow feel uplifting and cheerful.

(b)

The classic tones of natural wood and tan leather are so easy to live with.

(c)

Grey concrete walls paired with warm dark timber feels moody and cosy.

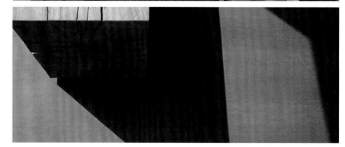

(d)

The colours of natural stone and brass.

(e)

Shades of warm white as a base to layer my collections.

Which is your preferred beach style?

(a)
NAUTICAL

(b)
NATURAL

(c)
WINTER

(d)
ELEVATED

(e)
BEACHCOMBER

Choosing a specific style can be a constructive way to visualise the beach vibe you lean towards. It sets a baseline for the look and feel you want to achieve. It can guide your tonal palette and the furnishings you select. Now, add in other tools to help amplify your style. Think of beach houses you admire; look at design magazines to gather images that appeal. Begin to nail down the specific elements that match your vision and shape your ideal beach style. As you start analysing interiors, you'll see similarities in what attracts you to a look. The vision for your space will gradually unfold.

What if you're drawn to elements of each style? Study the homes and interiors you like the most. Consider the mood of the space. Is there a strong energy or a quiet elegance in the room? Which design features are you drawn to? Is there a creative use of colour, a specific type of furniture or is it the way the room is composed? It's possible to marry styles but, first, reflect on which features will work best in your home. With careful planning and selection of colours, textures and furnishings, style elements can blend in a cohesive way.

THE FEEL

W hile defining your ultimate look is important, the feel and mood is a key element of your design. Take some time to think of words that capture how you want your beach house to look *and* feel.

Use these words, and think of others, to visualise your ideal space. Which materials will evoke the special mood you would like to create?

Grounded	Warm
Calm	Bright
Moody	Bohemian
Energised	Zen
Luxe	Minimal
Expansive	Restrained
Fresh	Beachy
Tropical	Relaxed
Cosy	Lively
Wintery	Marine
Airy	Bold
Cocooned	Striking

03.

01 Airiness. A feeling of uncluttered spaciousness; the walls are light in colour, but this is not a basic white. Polished plaster walls add a soft backdrop to layer more texture.

02 Tonal palette. This space unites a limited colour palette of warm whites, creams, soft greys with terracotta and timber tones to achieve a serene vibe. For a more dynamic feel, use contrasting colour in the room.

03 Pattern play. Though this space is calm, it still feels alive. An overscale pattern is used to great effect in the floor rug, playing with the geometry of the luxe central table.

04 Minimal maximalist. There is only one large modular sofa; nothing is superfluous, yet the rich textures and finishes make this space feel luxurious. It's a perfect balance of minimalism and maximalism.

05 Soft lines. When the architecture of a room leans to angular, straight lines, let the furniture provide softness. These rounded wall sconces and side table and 'bubbly' sofa conjure the foaming waters of the shoreline.

06 Framed. Grigio Firma marble lines the wall openings, clearly delineating the spaces. Rather than being an open plan area, this creates a sense of separation and a different feeling between lounge and dining rooms.

NAUTICAL

3.
Contrasting
Colours

1.
Energised

2.
Beachy

NATURAL

2.
Relaxed

1.
Grounded

3.
Earthy

WINTER

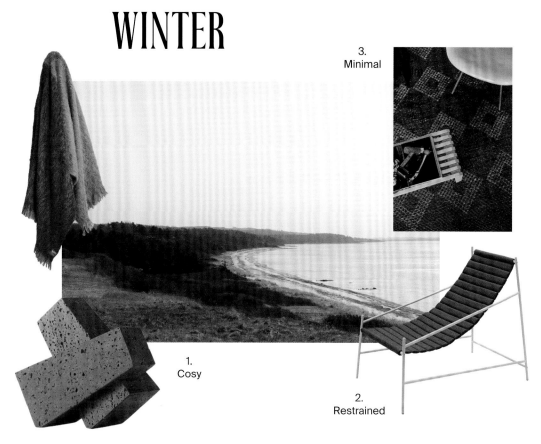

3.
Minimal

1.
Cosy

2.
Restrained

ELEVATED

1.
Luxe

2.
Airy

3.
Sumptuous

BEACHCOMBER

1.
Bohemian

2.
Lively

3.
Eclectic

THE PLAN

Transforming your space into the laid-back coastal home of your dreams can be a daunting process. If you're starting with an empty white room, it can seem almost impossible to achieve those beachy vibes.

You may be tempted to buy something big to fill that empty space, but don't. Occasionally a spur-of-the-moment purchase can work out, but often it results in costly mistakes – the rug is too small or the sofa too large. Perhaps the room lacks presence, or is filled with things that don't come together.

A design plan will keep you on track. It's a clear vision of what you are aiming for, and how you want the space to look and feel. Serendipitous magic can still occur, but with a plan in hand you can enjoy the experience and feel confident in your design direction.

A satisfying space doesn't happen in one weekend; an essential ingredient is time. When you're implementing the plan in a considered way, over time, design alchemy happens: your carefully chosen elements click, and the entire room comes together. Start by compiling a set of tools to build your plan.

INTERIOR PLANNING TOOLS

NOTEBOOK
Use this book as a guide, with sticky notes to flag image references. Write down key words that describe the feeling of the images you like.

IMAGE LIBRARY
Consider Pinterest or Instagram to store reference images, or simply use a folder on your computer for saved images. Look for images of beaches, architecture and fashion to build an idea of how you want your space to feel. The quality that attracts you to your chosen images and rooms may not be apparent at first; it could be the way they make you feel. You will begin to see commonalities in your images and then you can edit them down for a clear vision.

MOOD BOARD
Print out your edited images or tear out of magazines and use a pinboard to arrange them. This mood board helps you stay on track with your ideal space. Aim for no more than ten images.

MATERIALS
Gather materials. Start by visiting your beach or landscape and gather the shells, seaweed, driftwood, coloured glass and rocks (take a photo of them). This is the beginning of your materials palette. Then source the materials that form the base for your spaces.

FOLDERS
As you implement your design, use a digital folder or a binder to stay organised. Arrange in folders:

A. Images – as above, this may have subfolders per room.

B. Floor plans – for each room you are designing.

C. Schedules – a spreadsheet that lists the finishes, furniture and lighting with suppliers and prices.

D. Budget tracker – to allocate total spend, plus allowances per room or element.

E. Project plan – to track timeframes for renovations and deliveries. If your project is larger, software such as Trello or Asana is a great way to keep organised.

F. Management – for quotes and invoices.

With a plan at the ready, the design phase can begin. The images and styling material in this book can provide inspiration and guidance for your chosen look.

The Style Guide provides a catalogue of designers, artists, brands and products referenced throughout the book. Use it to trigger your imagination, begin the search for those special pieces and bring your own space to life.

It's time to start the design journey towards your Beachside Modern home.

THE STYLE GUIDE

This book features a diverse array of design concepts, objects, furnishings and accessories from inspiring designers, artists and brands. They range from aspirational looks and premium collectibles that are the stuff of dreams, to accessible styling ideas and objects that are readily available. The aim is to spark creativity when planning your space.

Beachside Modern is a versatile look that embraces both high-end and high street design and all points in between. Seek out objects that match your design vision from contemporary design shops, specialist vintage sites such as 1stDibs and Chairish, and purveyors of beach-inspired statement pieces, modern classics, original art and vintage treasures in your region.

For stylish, sustainable furnishings and objects, don't forget thrift shops; craft and second-hand markets and online marketplaces; antique dealers, auction houses and galleries. Source pieces that appeal to you, fit your design plan and budget, and evoke the beach style you are seeking.

More than anything, this list is intended to prompt exploration, evaluation and expression in pulling together your individual beach look.

Be inspired!

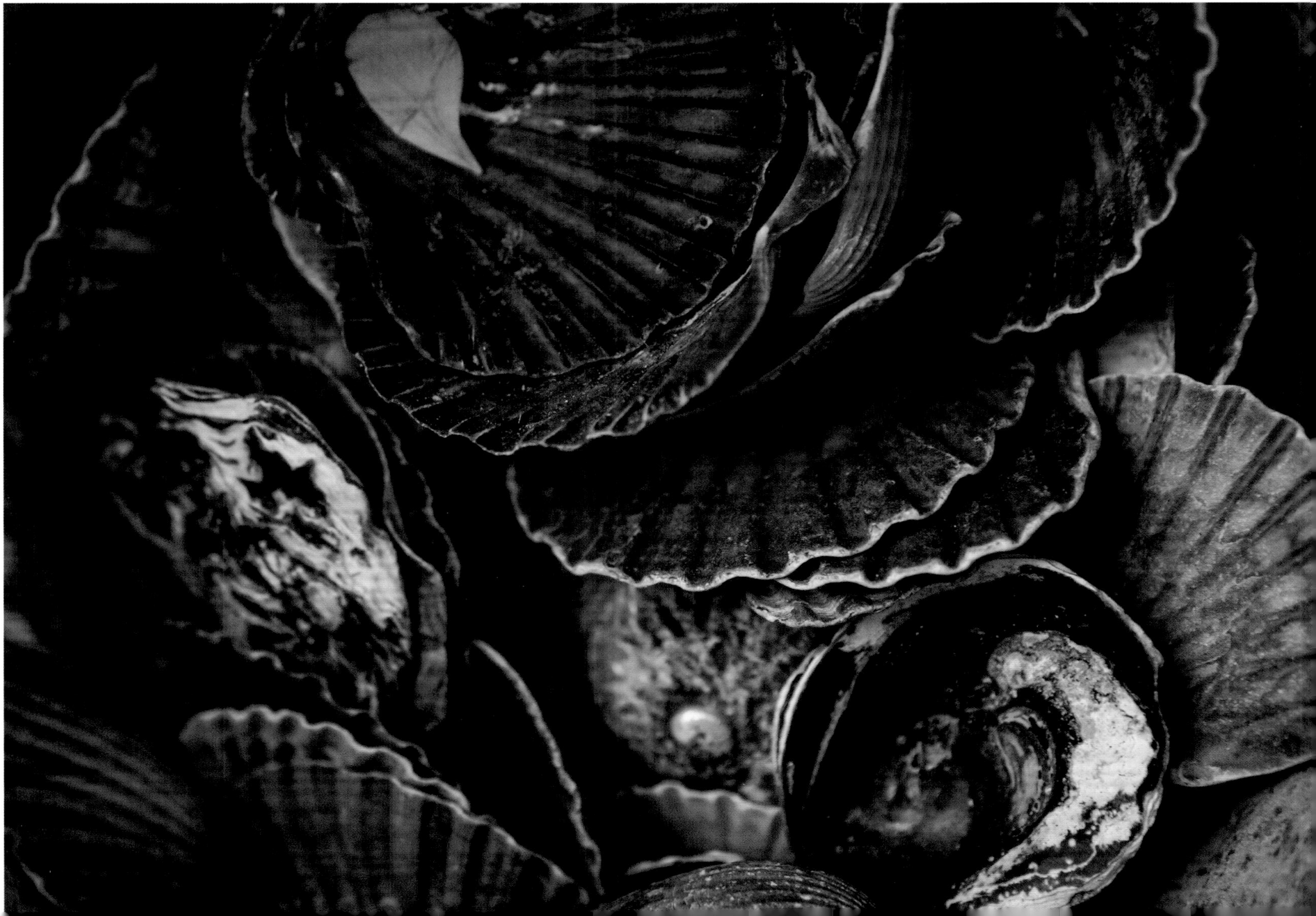

DESIGNERS

Alexander & Co

Amber Interiors

Andrew Burges Architects

Anna Spiro Design – Brisbane

APPARATUS

Architects EAT – Melbourne

ASHE LEANDRO – New York

Athena Calderone – New York

B&Co. Builders – New York

Bellhaus Design Office

Bestor Architecture – California

Betsy Brown – Alabama

Briony Fitzgerald Design

Bunsa Studio

Bureaux – South Africa

Christopher Boots – Melbourne

Claire Cousins Architects – Melbourne

Claire Delmar, STUDIO CD

Commune Design – Los Angeles

David Harrison and Karen McCartney

Dorothée Delaye Studio

Fearon Hay Architects – New Zealand

Feldman Architecture

Fiona Lynch Office – Melbourne

Georgina Jeffries – Victoria

Hommeboys – California

India Mahdavi – France

Jeremy Anderson APPARATUS

Kate Beadle Interior Design

Kelly Wearstler

Kennedy Nolan – Melbourne

Leanne Ford Interiors – Pennsylvania

Lynda Gardener – Melbourne

Manna Made

Michael Anastassiades

NICOLEHOLLIS – California

Nina Farmer Interiors

Norm Architects – Denmark

Pandolfini Architects

Reath Design Studio – California

Richard Unsworth

Romenek Design Studio

SARAH ANDREWS

Sarah Sherman Samuel

Sarah Solis Design Studio

Simon Couchman Architects

Simone Haag

Sisällä Studio

Stahl + Band

Studio LEESISAN

STUDIO LIFE/STYLE

Studioilse

Tobias Partners

Vico Magistretti

Vitra

Volker Haug Studio

SOURCES

&Tradition

1stDibs

Abode Living

APPARATUS

Armadillo

Ash NYC

bedouin SOCIETE

Beni Rugs

Besser Block

BYREDO

Chairish

Cole & Son

DesignByThem

Diptyque

Dowel Jones

Dulux

EDITIONS SERGE MOUILLE

EyeSwoon by Athena Calderone

FAINA

Flamingo Estate

Floral Street

GOLDEN EDITIONS

GUBI

Imprint House

Jan Murphy Gallery

Jan Vogelpoel

Jardan

Jatana Interiors

Jo Malone

Kazari

Kip&Co

Laminex

Ligne Roset

Living Divani

Marketplace (Facebook)

Marrakech Design

Marz Designs

Mitzi

MM Lampadari

Nemo Lighting

Pampa

PET Lamp

Pierre Frey

Pop & Scott

popham design

Porter's Paints

PP Møbler

Matter Made

SARAH ELLISON

Sika-Design

Spence & Lyda

Stahl + Band

STUDIO LIFE/STYLE

The Apartment – Denmark

The Dharma Door

The Galerie

Volker Haug Studio

WÄSTBERG

Workstead

FURNISHINGS

Akari Light Sculptures
by Isamu Noguchi at Vitra

Basket lounge chair by
Joe Colombo at GUBI

Beni Rugs

Bobby Bar Stool by
DesignByThem

BYREDO Altar Candle

Camaleonda sofa by Mario
Bellini for B&B Italia

Carimate chair by Vico
Magistretti for Casina, Italy

Cole & Son Acquario wallpaper

Diptyque candles

Dreamer Couch by Pop
and Scott

Dulux paints (Buff It, Natural
White, Henna Red, Happy, Sky
Eyes, Marais, Mount Buller)

Favela Chair by the
Campana Brothers

Flamingo Estate candles
(Euphoria, Clarity)

Flag Halyard chair designed
by Hans Wegner, made by
PP Møbler

Floral Street candle
Sunflower Pop

Issa Chandelier by
Tali Roth for Mitzi Lighting

Issa Wall Sconce by Tali Roth
for Mitzi

Jo Malone Wood Sage and
Sea Salt Home Candle

Knotty Bubbles Chain
Chandelier by Lindsey
Adelman Studio

Laminex Surround

Lamp de Marseilles by
Le Corbusier at Nemo Lighting

Lampadaire Droit by
Serge Mouille Editions

Little Petra by Vigo Boessen
at &Tradition

Multi-Lite by Louis Weisdorf
at GUBI

Murano glass

NeoWall sofa by Piero Lissoni
at Living Divani

Officina chair by Magis

PET Lamp by Spence & Lyda

Pierre Frey Poseidon wallpaper

Pillow Chair at Ash NYC

Porter's Paints (Smooth
Impasto, Interno Lime Wash)

Puffball by Faye Toogood for
Matter Made

Puna collection at Pampa

Revers Sofa by GUBI

SARAH ELLISON
(Pièrre chair | Muse)

Soriana Sofa by Afra and
Tobia Scarpa

STRIKHA by FAINA

Studioilse for Zanat

Togo by Michel Ducaroy
at Ligne Roset

Touch Table by Studioilse
for Zanat

w102 by David Chipperfield
at WÄSTBERG

Wall Sconce by Serge Mouille

Womb Chair by Eero Saarinen

ARTWORK CREDITS

ADDITIONAL IMAGE CREDITS

PAGE 5		Photographer: Jakob Owens (unsplash)
PAGE 6		Interior Designer: Commune Design; Photographer: Stephen Kent Johnson
PAGE 7		Photographer: Milly Mead
PAGE 8		Interior Designer: Dorothée Delaye Studio; Photographer: Mr. TRIPPER
PAGE 9		Interior Designer: Dorothée Delaye Studio; Photographer: Mr. TRIPPER
PAGE 10		Architect: Simon Couchman Architects; Interior Designer: Simone Haag; Photographer: Timothy Kaye
PAGE 12		Image courtesy of Ferm Living
PAGE 37	(01)	Image courtesy of Adam Lester and Jan Murphy Gallery
	(02)	Image courtesy of HAY
	(03)	Image courtesy of HAY
	(04)	Image courtesy of HAY
	(05)	Image courtesy of Skagerak
	(06)	Image courtesy of HAY
	(07)	Image courtesy of Audo Copenhagen
PAGE 75	(01)	Photographer: Ludovic Balay/Milk/Vega Mg
	(02)	Image courtesy of HK Living
	(03)	Image courtesy of Ferm Living
	(04)	Image courtesy of GUBI
	(05)	Image courtesy of Ferm Living
	(06)	Image courtesy of Ferm Living
	(07)	Image courtesy of SARAH ELLISON
PAGE 109	(01)	Image courtesy of WÄSTBERG
	(02)	Image courtesy of HK Living
	(03)	Image courtesy of HK Living
	(04)	Image courtesy of HK Living
	(05)	Image courtesy of Ferm Living
	(06)	Image courtesy of Zanat
	(07)	Image courtesy of HAY
PAGE 143	(01)	Image courtesy of HK Living
	(02)	Image courtesy of GUBI
	(03)	Image courtesy of Sancal
	(04)	Image courtesy of HK Living
	(05)	Image courtesy of SARAH ELLISON
	(06)	Image courtesy Jan Vogelpoel
PAGE 175	(01)	Image courtesy of HK Living
	(02)	Image courtesy of Ferm Living
	(03)	Image courtesy of HK Living
	(04)	Image courtesy of Ferm Living
	(05)	Image courtesy of Zanat
	(06)	Image courtesy of Ferm Living
PAGE 196		Interior Designer: Kate Beadle Interior Design; Photographer: Nikole Ramsay
PAGE 200	(A)	Photographer: Yiorgos Ntrahas (unsplash)
	(B)	Photographer: Harold Wainwright (unsplash)
	(C)	Photographer: Tim Trad (unsplash)
	(D)	Photographer: Marius Cern (unsplash)
	(E)	Photographer: Sarah Brown (unsplash)
PAGE 201	(A)	Pillow Chair by Ash NYC Image courtesy of Ash NYC
	(B)	Basket lounge chair by GUBI Image courtesy of GUBI
	(C)	Shearling armchair Image courtesy of Audo Copenhagen
	(D)	Float by SARAH ELLISON Image courtesy of SARAH ELLISON

	(E)	GUBI Grace Lounge Chair Image courtesy of GUBI
PAGE 202	(A)	Image courtesy of Sage x Clare
	(B)	Photographer: Bree Anne (unsplash)
	(C)	Photographer: Olesia Bahrii (unsplash)
	(D)	Photographer: Taisiia Shestopale (unsplash)
	(E)	Photographer: Sarah Youthed (unsplash)
PAGE 203	(A)	Photographer: Kelly Russo (unsplash)
	(B)	Photographer: Stephanie Green (unsplash)
	(C)	Photographer: Sergei Solo (unsplash)
	(D)	Image courtesy of Audo Copenhagen
	(E)	Photographer: Neom (unsplash)
PAGE 204	(A)	Image courtesy of HAY
	(B)	Image courtesy of Fredericia Furniture
	(C)	Photographer: Jonas Bjerre-Poulsen
	(D)	Image courtesy of Audo Copenhagen
	(E)	Image courtesy of HK Living
PAGES 206–207		Interior Designer: Alexander & Co; Styling: Claire Delmar; Photographer: Anson Smart
PAGE 212		Image courtesy of Skagerak
PAGE 215		Interior Designer: SARAH ANDREWS.; Photographer: Lean Timms
PAGE 222		Interior Designer: Alexander & Co; Styling: Claire Delmar; Photographer: Anson Smart

PHOTOGRAPHERS

Thank you to the talented photographers whose images have brought these interiors to life.

ADAM POTTS	@ADAMPOTTSPHOTO
ANSON SMART	@SMARTANSON
BRIGID ARNOTT	@BRIGIDARNOTTPHOTOGRAPHY
CRICKET SALEH	@CRICKETSALEH_
ERIC ROTH	@ERICROTHPHOTO
FERM LIVING	@FERMLIVING
JONAS BJERRE-POULSEN	@JONASBJERREPOULSEN
KAREL BALAS / MILK / VEGA MG	@KAREL_BALAS
LEAN TIMMS	@LEANTIMMS
MILLY MEAD	@MILLYMEAD
MR. TRIPPER	@MISTER_TRIPPER
NICOLE FRANZEN	@NICOLE_FRANZEN
NIKOLE RAMSAY	@NIKOLERAMSAY
RORY GARDINER	@ARORYGARDINER
SIMON WILSON	SIMONWILSON.CO.NZ
SKAGERAK	@SKAGERAK
STEPHEN KENT JOHNSON	@STEPHENKENTJOHNSON
TESS KELLY	@TESSKELLYPHOTOGRAPHY
THE INGALLS	@INGALLSPHOTO
TIMOTHY KAYE	@TIMOTHYKAYE

ENDNOTES

1   Martin Genberg, 'The Swedes and their summer house',
    6 September 2022, *Visit Sweden*, viewed 3 December 2022,
    <visitsweden.com/what-to-do/culture-history-and-art/culture/lifestyle/
    swedes-summer-house/>

2   Janet Abbott, 'The Kiwi Bach', 9 November 2018, *hut2hut*,
    viewed 3 December 2022,
    <hut2hut.info/the-kiwi-bach-new-zealand-vernacular-architecture/>

ACKNOWLEDGEMENTS

Interior design won't change the world, but it can change *your* world. Creating a space that fills you with joy is truly worthwhile.

We each have a different vision for our own home – I don't subscribe to one 'look' – and I hope that you feel inspired by the special beach houses in this book. So, thank you dear reader for coming along with me. And to my design community, thanks for your support and encouragement.

Writing a book is by no means a solitary undertaking. It is a true collaboration. There are so many people who have made this book happen. Thank you, Rachel Carter and Paulina de Laveaux at Thames & Hudson, for your clever ideas, and your belief in me and this book. Sally Holdsworth has not only lent her brilliant, thoughtful editing but is an encouraging voice throughout, elevating my words and being the ultimate sounding board. I'm so thrilled that Evi-O Studio has worked its creative magic on this book. It's absolutely beautiful.

Lucy Feagins of *The Design Files*, thank you for giving me the opportunity to write for your innovative, influential publication. It is an honour.

I've loved working with designers around the world to compile this book. Your passion to push the boundaries in interior design is inspiring. Much gratitude to Austin and Alex (Hommeboys), Andrew (Andrew Burgess Architects), Athena (Athena Calderone), Betsy (Betsy Brown), Briony (Briony Fitzgerald Design), Dani (Manna Made), Dominic (Pandolfini Architects), Dorothée Delaye (Dorothée Delaye Studio), Georgina (Georgina Jeffries), Gianni (Vega MG), Jennifer (Bunsa Studio), Jonas (Norm Architects), Kate (Kate Beadle Interior Design), Kate (Fearon Hay Architects), Kelly (Kelly Wearstler), Natasha (Natasha Allen Creative), Nick Tobias (Tobias Partners), Nina (Nina Farmer Interiors), Richard (Richard Unsworth), Roman and Steven (Commune Design), Sarah Andrews, Simone (Simone Haag) and Tess (Alexander & Co).

The beautiful photographs in this book showcase stylish and diverse beach house interiors, but more than that, they capture the spirit and atmosphere of these coastal homes.

I'd also like to thank my husband, Phil. We've created a wonderful life together since we met on that revolving dance floor. You're completely present in our family life, and you wholeheartedly support every idea I have for our business and in writing this book. Your belief in me gives me the courage to keep going and I am so grateful. Indigo, Coco and Benji, you are my greatest motivation. Thank you to the best uncle in the world, William, your support is incredible. And to Mum, thank you for always creating a beautiful home that instilled in me how our spaces can affect the way we feel.

ABOUT THE AUTHOR

Lauren Li is the founding director of Melbourne interior design studio Sisällä, born of a passion to create beautifully rich spaces reflective of her clients' contexts, lifestyles and individual desires. She has more than twenty years of experience across the residential, retail and commercial sectors, specialising in high-end residential and conceptual design; space planning; interior decoration; selection of finishes, fixtures and furniture; and project management. Sisällä's projects have been recognised by several awards programs, including the Australian Interior Design Awards, and as a five-time finalist of *House & Garden*'s Top 50 Rooms. She is a trusted mentor to interior designers inside a community called The Design Society and is a regular contributor to *The Design Files*. *Beachside Modern* is the second book in the Style Study series, following *The New French Look*.

First published in Australia in 2024
by Thames & Hudson Australia Pty Ltd
11 Central Boulevard, Portside Business Park
Port Melbourne, Victoria 3207
ABN: 72 004 751 964

First published in the United Kingdom
in 2024 by Thames & Hudson Ltd
181a High Holborn
London WCIV 7QX

First published in the United States
of America in 2024 by Thames & Hudson Inc.
500 Fifth Avenue
New York, New York 10110

Beachside Modern
© Thames & Hudson Australia 2024

Text © Lauren Li 2024
Images © copyright in all texts, artworks
and images is held by the creators or their
representatives, unless otherwise stated.

27 26 25 24   5 4 3 2 1

The moral right of the author has been asserted.

All rights reserved. No part of this publication
may be reproduced or transmitted in any form
or by any means, electronic or mechanical,
including photocopy, recording or any other
information storage or retrieval system, without
prior permission in writing from the publisher.

Any copy of this book issued by the publisher
is sold subject to the condition that it shall not
by way of trade or otherwise be lent, resold,
hired out or otherwise circulated without the
publisher's prior consent in any form or binding
or cover other than that in which it is published
and without a similar condition including these
words being imposed on a subsequent purchaser.

Thames & Hudson Australia wishes to
acknowledge that Aboriginal and Torres Strait
Islander people are the first storytellers of
this nation and the Traditional Custodians
of the land on which we live and work. We
acknowledge their continuing culture and
pay respect to Elders past and present.

ISBN 978-1-760-76334-3
ISBN 978-1-760-76423-4 (U.S. edition)

British Library Cataloguing-in-Publication Data
A catalogue record for this book is available
from the British Library

A catalogue record for this
book is available from the
National Library of Australia

Library of Congress Control Number
2023941562

Every effort has been made to trace accurate
ownership of copyrighted text and visual
materials used in this book. Errors or omissions
will be corrected in subsequent editions,
provided notification is sent to the publisher.

Front cover:
Trincomalee, Pittwater residence of
landscape designer, Richard Unsworth
Photographer: Anson Smart

Design: Evi-O.Studio | Evi O, Emi Chiba
& Susan Le, Matthew Crawford
Editing: Sally Holdsworth
Printed and bound in China by
C&C Offset Printing Co. Ltd

FSC® is dedicated to the promotion
of responsible forest management worldwide.
This book is made of material from FSC®-
certified forests and other controlled sources.

Be the first to know about our new releases,
exclusive content and author events by visiting
thamesandhudson.com.au
thamesandhudson.com
thamesandhudsonusa.com